Table of Contents

HELP!

My Emotions Are Out of Control

A holistic mental health guide to managing your emotions
Dr. Carolyn Prince

ISBN: 9798215428160

Dedication

I dedicate this book to my parents, Jacob and Eunice Prince.

I saw their dedication in raising their young family and doing the best they could with the resources they had, given their own trauma-profile history. My siblings (Hanzel, Dianne, and Yvonne) and I were all affected in one way or the other by our parents' trauma profile, which invariably affected our childhood experiences and consequently impacted our perspective of life and relationships.

My youngest sister, Yvonne, and both my parents are now deceased. However, my parents' impact remains in the way it affects two of my favorite people in the world, Hanzel and Dianne. My desire is that we continue to grow, heal and inspire each other to thrive and flourish in our quest for abundant mental health.

About the Author

Dr. Prince is a Licensed Naturopathic Medical Doctor (NMD), and a Licensed Mental Health Counselor (LMHC). She completed both her under-grad and master's degrees in Psychology and Counseling respectively and continued on to earn her Naturopathic Medical Degree (NMD).

Dr. Prince is passionate about helping people live the best versions of themselves and has a laser focus on bringing about health and healing so that patients/clients may bud, flourish and live fully functioning lives. Dr. Prince holds that human beings are not just a physical body and approaches her work with the mindset of finding and identifying the root cause of current dysfunction, negative belief systems, and maladaptive behaviors that add sabotage and bring chaos to people's lives. Dr. Prince believes that becoming authentic and whole, as a human being, in large part, involves addressing past unresolved traumas, and integrating the physical, mental, emotional, and spiritual aspects of our lives is a crucial part of her work.

Dr. Prince describes that her fire is lit when she has opportunities to integrate the modalities of Naturopathic medicine with mental health. It literally "floats my boat," she says. Dr. Prince uses a combination of modalities, including CBT, DBT, EMDR, MEMI, Mindfulness practices, Acupuncture, Botanical Medicine, Diet/lifestyle training & Homeopathy to restore the beauty of wholeness and well-being.

Dr. Prince credits her faith in Jesus to do this work and depends on and utilizes Biblical wisdom to access clarity, understanding, and knowledge on how to exquisitely interact with patients/clients/people so that, in the end, they benefit.

Preface

Health is our number one wealth. Money is secondary to health. Health embraces our physical, spiritual, and mental-emotional spheres. It is imperative that we maintain good health and do everything within our power to stay healthy.

When asked what health is or what are the requirements of staying healthy, we are quick to point toward options that indicate physical well-being. For most people, maintaining physical health and being mindful of our diet and physical activities is the only way to stay healthy. Though reality includes physical health, it does not exclude other parts of our being. There are many other aspects to staying healthy, and we shall uncover and learn about them as we read more.

Page Left Blank Intentionally

Chapter 1 — Introduction

"I am not afraid of storms, for I am learning how to sail my ship."

—Louisa May Alcott, 1868

Mental health is finally getting the attention it deserves. Everywhere you turn, you can find somebody talking about their mental health. It has become part of the news cycle, talk shows, and podcasts alike. In the course of the past years, the conversation around mental health has taken a turn for the better. The dark shadows of the stigma that once lurked around all discussions surrounding mental health continue to wither away with the passage of time.

However, in some major cultures of our country of birth or micro-cultures in our individual families, the narrative about mental health is hardly examined. Often the negative view of mental health is based on some erroneous worldview or unresolved personal trauma. But when there is a change in the distorted thought patterns, or when we adjust our mindsets or perspective, we will discover that mental and emotional health is available to all. For most of us, the prospect of a satisfying life seems like a distant dream, and the implausibility of it all prevents us from even trying to improve. But no matter how distant or futile our attempts might seem to date; I encourage you that your effort is worth it to achieve the goal of mental health.

Today, while there is still a long way to go, the environment of the world is one where stigmas and taboos surrounding mental health are no longer the centers of attention. For the most part, the shame has largely dissipated like dew on a hot triple-digit summer day. As the conversation progresses, both professionals and lay people are now more eager than ever to seek mental health counseling to address issues that hinder their daily lives, including anxiety, depression, stress, PTSD, panic attacks, trauma, or relationship issues. Often, individuals opt for counseling sessions to sort through the traumas from their past or unresolved childhood issues and to open for themselves pathways to healing and a better, or more fulfilled life.

Mental health is as important as our physical health. It is an integral part of who we are as human beings. Achieving wholeness and healing in our mental and emotional lives is a process that can be accomplished with intentional work and commitment to change.

As mentioned above, although the conversation surrounding mental health has significantly improved over the past years, there is still a long way to go. Ideally, mental health counseling should be offered to everyone, equally, around the globe, but certainly, this isn't the case. While mental health counseling is more prevalent in developed countries, there is still a lot to be desired as far as the rest of the world goes.

In the developed world, great strides have been made to ensure the availability of mental health expertise to all. And progress is seen when both the young and the elderly have access to and receive support for mental health services. In that regard, I really do believe that achieving and maintaining mental and emotional health strengthens generations throughout their lifespans and fosters an environment in which love, joy, peace, patience, goodness, kindness, and gentleness toward self and others can flourish.

I sincerely believe that human beings need other positive human beings to be fully human, and if we are to get emotional healing both as individuals and as a people — we cannot do it by ourselves and on our own.

We need community. We develop and become wholesome human beings in the company of other loving and nurturing human beings. We were not created to be alone or to live in isolation. We cannot experience mental health in the total and complete absence of other people, and neither can we live an abundant life in a vacuum without a community. At our core, humans are social beings; therefore, we cannot survive, flourish or thrive in our own cocoons or in isolation. We need at least one other human being to bear witness to our lives, to see us, to accept us, and to love us with our scars, dimples, cellulites, and all.

As much as some may enjoy being alone and finding solace away from the crowd, we cannot flourish by ourselves ad-infinitum. Having human relationships is key to being fully human. What I'm not saying is that every relationship is a healthy one. As a matter of fact, it may be healthier not to welcome certain individuals in our heart space.

We can indeed love them from afar as fellow human beings and be kind and gracious to them when our paths intersect, but inviting them out for tea or coffee or into our homes may not foster or contribute to our mental health and well-being; so it is better to keep these individuals on the periphery of our social lives.

What I am saying, however, is that as an adult, it is our social task and goal to find good, healthy, and positive relationships and to maintain and nurture these because it is in these types of healthy relationships that our own mental health flourishes. Naturally, this takes time to test whether one relationship is a keeper and the other is not. Having a minimum of one positive friendship over a lifetime is a blessing.

Living abundant lives seem foreign to many. We understand and embrace the grind and hustle as normal. Being busy and always being on the go seems to be an esteemed status quo for some, but this "always on the go " mentality is not sustainable. The challenge is to make room and intentionally put margins in our lives to focus on attaining mental health and well-being.

The fostering of our mental health, or the lack of it, starts with the first human relationships we experience within our family of origin. Some may describe their childhood as good and their parents the best they could have asked for. Yet, for others, it is quite the opposite. Our parents, all things being equal, did the best they could, and as adults, we carry the wounds that they've either knowingly or unknowingly inflicted upon us. Parents also have their trauma profile of anxieties of past-unresolved emotional issues that, by default, they contribute to their children's lives.

An ancient sacred text in I Corinthians 13:11 says,

"When I was a child, I spoke as a child, I understood as a child, I thought as a child: but when I became a man, I put away childish things."

As adults, we develop a level of sophistication in pretense or a façade to hide our childish ways. If we were honest with ourselves, we would find that we still wrestle with the same childish issues in our day-to-day lives. The tragedy I find is that we are not able to correlate childish ways to some unresolved issues that morphed into our adult experience. No matter how in earnest we try to sweep these issues under the proverbial rug, it often seems to be the same unresolved issues we didn't have the capacity or language to deal with as children, ultimately resurfacing and wreaking havoc in our personal, social, and professional lives.

With each birthday, we can measure our growth spurt. We grow taller and stronger and look healthy physically. Men look at the outside appearance and give a verdict of approval with statements and questions like "you look so good!

Are you exercising? Are you on a diet?" and so on. What is deceiving is that nobody has the type of eyes to see the soul, which is the house of our emotional being; we don't see the emotionally stunted child within us. So that while we look good on the outside, we are still struggling with the wounded and traumatized child trapped in a fetal position in our adult bodies. The grit your teeth and bear it mentality or the suck it up or stuff it down mindset is not sustainable simply because it requires an enormous amount of emotional energy from our internal mental resources to maintain the façade of faking being good mentally. However, none among us have an infinite internal emotional capacity, and so when our emotional resources get drained, we are left depleted.

Make no mistake about it, some people have maintained the façade for years and even decades, and the moment a tragedy or crisis or simply when exhaustion catches up with them, the emotional wounded-ness resurfaces in a way that humbles us all. It seems as if the trauma was just one small step behind, nipping at our ankles all those years and decades. When we do not do the emotional work to address the unresolved childhood emotional bruises or wounds, then the childish, immature perspective and mentality persists in our adult lives and relationships. The type of emotional work we all need to do in earnest doesn't escape any of us. We all have to do our work to achieve mental health and remain emotionally healthy.

For the sake of honesty, however, I'd like to raise a question. Haven't we all been guilty of putting more emphasis and attention on our physical appearance? We place emphasis on the clothes we wear, the shoes we put on, the hair we straighten, curl, braid, or weave, and the matted makeup, which is a work of art that covers or hides some undesirable feature on our face. We look good, we smell good, and from all appearances, we believe we are well when we step out in the world. We take care of ourselves from the outside-to enhance our physical appearance, but what about our mental health? Just like we would take care of our physical health, we also need to pay close attention to our mental health. Our mental/emotional life does not offer us an option or an alternative to neglecting it. It is a priority and a necessity to take care of our mental health, which may include seeking support from a mental health professional to address the woundedness or brokenness of our mental/emotional life.

Living without wholesome mental health is analogous to walking on a three-inch heel on your right foot and a flat sneaker on your left foot, resulting in an uneven and unsteady gait, which causes you to trip, stumble and get a nasty tumble after a few steps.

No matter how great your life is on the outside, if you keep repressing trauma, emotional woundedness, stress, anxiety, or depression, cracks will ultimately appear. Even if you go decades without placing adequate and appropriate emphasis on mental/emotional health care, things fall apart, and the struggles we face eventually overwhelm our capacity to deal with the situation at hand.

This book is a gateway to help you understand that everyone, even the best among us, goes through our fair share of hardships, trials, and traumas. And to let you know you are not alone in this world. Despite what your mind might be telling you, the help and support you need to overcome your trauma and achieve mental health is available as you reach out and ask for help.

Mental health is not superior to physical health or vice versa. We simply need to nourish our mental/emotional health like we nourish our physical health, as we would consume meals or snacks throughout the day to provide nourishment for physical sustenance and energy. Similarly, we have to nourish our mental/emotional health with intentional practices to sustain, nourish and nurture our emotional being.

And so, the question becomes, how do you nourish and nurture your emotional being to maintain mental health? That is a great question that I seek to address in offering this book.

My intention for writing this book is to counsel those I may never meet and to let them know that the journey they have undertaken to care for and nourish their mental/emotional life is a noble one. It is to offer you those skills-sets and tools that I've invited my clients to implement into their daily lives. I hope that you will find what I share to be practical and useful in making a difference in your mental health journey.

As the world grows more open and empathetic, there is no better time than now to get the help you need. Consider this book your own personal counselor, trainer, cheerleader, and coach. I'm in your corner, showing you how to achieve mental and emotional health.

Chapter 2 — Body, Soul, and Spirit

"And sometimes I have kept my feelings to myself because I could find no language to describe them in."

— Jane Austen, 1811

I believe we are triune beings and not just physical bodies. We have a Soul and a Spirit, and they live in our physical bodies. Our spirit is the essence of who we are. And our soul is the mental and emotional part of our being. It is the thinking, feeling, and choosing part of our being. It's the part where memories are stored and from where our deepest desires and emotions arise; hence, it needs quiet, restful, and unrushed time often in nature, to be restored, refreshed, and revitalized.

I like to think that our souls are full of thoughts, emotions, choices, and memories, and these align with our spirit to communicate and interact with the world using the body as the interface. I have heard it said that our existence on this planet is our spirit having a human experience in a physical world.

We use our five physical senses: sight, hearing, smell, taste, and touch, to navigate this physical world. We get information from these physical senses' portals. We understand where we are in the world and how we interact with everything in it. We live in this world as fish live in water, thinking that there is no other medium but water. Some people believe that this physical world is all that exists and everything around us is only physical nature. But when we encounter a challenge to this worldview, we recognize that there is more to life than what we see, feel and experience in the physical realm.

However, our physical body is important. It occupies space and time and also locates us. We are in one place at a single time. Our bodies come in all shapes and sizes, and to grow physically healthy, we need to tend to the body's needs and care for it by healthy eating habits, sleeping well, and having movement or exercise in our routines to give the body what it needs to thrive.

If we start with the premise that our parents did their best in raising us and that they were good parents, then it may be safe to say that they, too, had a good childhood. But we all know that many would describe their childhood as difficult or even traumatic, infused with abuse, abandonment, and emotional trauma.

To put things into perspective, a great place to start is acknowledging this simple fact: we all survived childhood. Our parents fed and clothed us, and that seemed enough. Perhaps not with 5-course meals crafted by the best personal chefs; or perhaps we did not have designer clothes or shoes or lived in a modern-day castle or mansion. But we surely can say that we had something to eat and wear, had a roof over our heads, and all the basic things we needed for our physical nourishment to grow normally. With each birthday, we looked physically well because we got that physical nourishment.

We can recognize when someone is malnourished, recalling images of undernourished kids with swollen bodies, thin limbs, and sunken eyes. It seems clear that they are physically malnourished. As a consequence, we engage in protective measures to give physical nourishment to such people.

Just like our physical being needs physical nourishment/food, clothes, and shelter, our emotional being needs it too. Our soul needs emotional nourishment.

Emotional nourishment and nurturing are essential for emotional well-being. Suppose our younger selves did not get the appropriate emotional nourishment for our souls. Then, in that case, we tend to grow up emotionally malnourished, layering it up with the traumas throughout our childhood. In such circumstances, our souls become flash-frozen at the point in time it was rudely impacted by the trauma, and we carry that trauma-scarred experience into adult life until it is processed and healed.

Unresolved trauma from the past will haunt us in both the present and the future; we can't go fast enough or far enough to get away from it. The intensity of the trauma of the soul becomes pressurized in our physical bodies and affects us in negative and harmful ways.

If we sustain a wound or black and blue bruise, we can see it on our physical bodies, and a scar develops where the wound once was after the injury has healed. When the wound is fully healed, we can apply deep pressure to it and not re-injure ourselves. However, when the wound is not fully healed from the inside out, applying deep pressure can potentially re-traumatize it.

Similarly, when we are emotionally triggered by something someone says or does or something they didn't say or do, we can overreact in a way that doesn't correspond to the initial infraction. The overreaction itself is an indication that something in the past is affecting the present. In other words, we re-traumatized an emotional wound that had not been properly healed. We walk around, figuratively limping, with our soul's wounds inflicted by past traumas.

The unresolved trauma and its emotional response stay hidden in some parts of our physical bodies. And when the trauma is triggered or reactivated, we get a range of physical symptoms, including but not limited to the following:

A knot in our stomach
Chest tightening
Lump in our throat
Dry mouth
A quiver in our voice
Trembling body

Two people may have different profiles of symptoms. But we cannot escape the fact that our emotions have a physical address in our physical bodies. Just like you have a physical home address where you receive your mail or packages, your emotions have a physical address, where they reside in your physical body. It is there where the negative charge of the unresolved trauma remains stuck or stagnated unless and until they get processed, unstuck, and released. If we could visibly see our souls, we would be able to see the cuts, bruises, and wounds knitted into its very fabric.

We would witness our souls curled up in a fetal position, weakened by the assaults of trauma and damage to the dignity, integrity, and self-esteem that we sustained over a lifetime. Almost like a frightened child curled up in a defensive position, co-existing as part of our physical being.

Just imagine with me for a moment that your frightened younger version of self is stunted and curled up because of the impact of some trauma or negative experiences, and this is happening simultaneously while we continue to grow physically, go to school, college, or work, get married, have children, and maintain a family, all the while, looking healthy by all external standards. It's like our bodies and souls are not integrated; we feel as if we are not really in our bodies. There is a breach, and we experience mental chaos, dissonance, and constant soul irritation because of it.

No human being would have a clue by simply looking at the physical features that you're walking around wounded and emotionally unhealthy because we do not have eyes to see the soul. We see the physical body, but we do not see our souls.

Now imagine if you were hurt and wounded from a trauma in your childhood and remained flash-frozen in that time and space in your psyche; it is understandable and quite reasonable that the unhealed trauma can produce a lop-sided perspective of life which then creates a domino effect in the way we navigate life and relationships. The perspective from which we see life is influenced by our childhood's hurt, pain, and dysfunctional template. And as a consequence, it is this weakened and wounded version of our lives that shows up in our perceptions and how we relate to others in our relationships with family, friends, colleagues, and life in general.

The way we view the world, and our relationships are molded into the shape of our wounded souls. Our perspective is shaped by our early emotional malnourishment and childhood traumas. This lop-sided emotional life is not sustainable, and we simply cannot live with that imbalance, at least not without facing mental/emotional consequences in our lives. The fallacy that we can somehow live fully with an immature and malnourished soul is erroneous. We simply cannot sustain a healthy emotional life in a lop-sided fashion.

Even when parents do the best they can, their parenting style can still inflict some emotional bruise or wound that continues to fester in our souls from our single-digit years to our adolescence uncertainties to our teenage awkwardness, and then arrive into our young adulthood and beyond with some deformed caricature of ourselves.

Parents are bound to make mistakes because they are human beings too, with their own trauma profile from their childhood and with which they parent their children. This is how the tragic cycle of generational hurt spirals into patterns and pitfalls of emotional immaturity, carrying on to the next child, the next life, and the next household.

How do we break this cycle? How do we interrupt the pattern? How do we begin to think differently, and how do we begin to truly heal our souls?

Giving our parents credit for all the things they did right is a good place to start. We remember eating meals because good parents provide physical nourishment. Think of it like this: At least we ate; even if it had been rice and beans, TV dinners, or fast foods, nonetheless, we ate. Our bodies grew taller and stronger with each birthday. At best, we had some form of shelter, even though it was not a castle, and we wore clothes and shoes even if they had holes in them or were second-hand from thrift stores or hand-me-downs.

So what's the problem? Well, for one thing, most parents didn't know how to care for and feed the soul or the spirit. And make no mistake about this; these areas needed nourishment as much as our physical bodies did.

Even if our parents didn't nourish us emotionally, there is still hope for us. As adults, we can assume the responsibility of re-parenting our younger selves and extending compassion by self-soothing those wounded parts of our emotional being. We have to become conscious and intentional so that we can recognize the patterns that produce dysfunctional behaviors and habits. We have to make a change. One simple change and do one thing differently. We have to change our perspective to acknowledge and recognize the hurt that our wounded younger selves sustained and offer compassion to that hurting younger version of our soul.

We can only change ourselves. We can only take responsibility for our decisions and must begin to nurture and do the emotional work to heal ourselves.

When we develop another set of eyes for the soul and become intentional about emotional soul-care, then, we begin the authentic journey of becoming whole and emotionally healthy.

This emotional nourishment work takes time, and it is possible to achieve. To begin healing that brokenness in your soul, you must first understand that your body, soul, and spirit are interconnected.

An undernourished or unhealed soul remains in a fetal position within us. Hence, even a physically grown adult, in whatever decade of their life, could still be living from an immature, childish perspective because the unhealed trauma marinates us and seeps into all aspects of our life, relationships, and decisions.

If you didn't get the desired nourishment for your mental health and emotional well-being throughout your childhood, there is still a tangible hope that is available for you to achieve emotional and mental health in the way you re-parent yourself. You can re-parent yourself once you realize your need for emotional nourishment.

I intend to show you in practical and useful ways how you can begin to re-parent yourself with new skill sets that can be applied to your daily life to achieve the mental health you desire and deserve.

Getting the help, you deserve requires intentional nourishment for your body, soul, and spirit.

We also need to take care of our spirit. The effort applied in caring for our souls is also needed by our spirits. You are mistaken if you think that the spirit doesn't exist because you can't see it. There are many things that you can't see, but they do exist. Moreover, it is often the things you can't see that play a vital role in our lives. For instance, electromagnetic waves, or radio waves, we know they exist because we use them to communicate electronically to others thousands of miles away within seconds through our smartphones or some other electronic device, but we cannot see these energy systems with our physical eyes.

We can't see the wind, and we don't know where it starts and where it ends, but we feel refreshed by a cool breeze in a hot summer. We can't see or even hold the wind in our hands, but we know it exists and can feel its effect.

Questions about life on earth or life after death, or how did the first humans come to live on this planet; what our life's purpose is, where do we go when we die; and is there a benevolent, good, kind, and compassionate Creator, are indeed the yearning and questions of our spirit. We need to understand and acknowledge the role of our spirit in our mental health and human existence. Faith is an invaluable resource for our mental health. Although I said 'faith', there may be some who would have heard what I didn't say and immediately got defensive. I didn't say religion is a valuable resource for mental health. Religion cannot represent God as it is often divisive and inflicts such deep hurt that drills into our souls. There are too many precious individuals who have been hurt by religion, and my heart aches for them because they neglect their spirit because of some form of religiosity.

Healing this type of hurt is crucial for integrating our body, soul, and spirit. Developing a well-rounded spiritual life has at its base the understanding that there is a good, kind, loving, and compassionate Creator-God, who takes the time to intricately know you in the way he numbered each strand of hair on your head. It is true. Believing this truth helps and supports your mental health. Some prefer to believe the error through the lens of the pain religion inflicted by perhaps someone in leadership in the church, synagogue, or mosque. But if you ask me, I will relate my experience of a God who seeks to come into a personal relationship with us to show Himself in tangible ways of love that we can appreciate. He is not a celestial grump waiting for you to mess up and bop you over the head with a really big hammer. That has been a lie that contributes to the emptiness some experience and seeks to fill with any drug of choice or mind-numbing excessive activity.

I started this chapter echoing my belief that we are triune beings; we have a body, soul, and spirit. If my premise is reasonable, we need to dig deep and find out the origin of the distress and dysfunction that permeates our very being. Does it originate in the body? Is it a physical problem? Is it a mental-emotional issue with the root cause residing in the soul? Or does our distress require a spiritual intervention?

Finding the root cause of recurring emotional problems or challenges is important because it sets us on a path to finding the most appropriate solution. As an integrated triune human being (three in one — body, soul, spirit), we can then understand how dysfunction in one area of our being affects the other areas; and so finding the root cause of the dysfunction and addressing the problem would lead to authentic and genuine healing for our total well-being. The alternative is to keep repeating dysfunctional patterns and remain superficial, like putting a band-aid on a deep puncture wound. It won't work; it never will, just like cutting a branch off a tree doesn't prevent it from producing fruits. It will continue producing new branches, leaves, and fruits because the hidden root system remains intact. It is my intention to help you dig deep into the root systems to effect significant and positive change for emotional health.

Chapter 3 — Anxiety and Depression

Anxiety and depression are the two most predominant mental health disorders in the United States and also worldwide. It interchanges sometimes but not very often; sometimes anxiety takes the lead, and other times depression does. The pandemic of 2020 and the subsequent shutdown seem to bring anxiety and depression into sharp focus, with people experiencing elevated levels of each. Those with a propensity to experience anxiety saw increased levels beyond their capacity to manage it. And those who experienced depression saw the depth of melancholy deteriorating into clinical depression.

The most recent COVID-19 pandemic underscored the notion that humans need other human beings to be fully human. We need other human beings to give witness to our lives so that we feel seen, heard, acknowledged, and validated.

We are not intended to live in isolation. Even though sometimes we feel that isolation is what we need, it is not a sustainable option. Because the moment we enter into isolation, we desire connection. Humans can't dwell in absolute isolation. We are not designed like that.

We cannot survive, much less thrive, by being disconnected and separated from our fellow men.

It absolutely makes sense why the isolation of the worldwide shutdown with restrictive travel and border closure took a toll on our mental health. Now that things have settled into a new normal, the hope is that a new appreciation for being a part of the community is sustained.

In this chapter, I intend to give you language and help you understand some mental-health symptoms you might have experienced or are currently experiencing. I will offer practical actions on how you can care for your emotional being.

Anxiety is a subset of fear. Fear is one of the basic emotions. I would reiterate the four basic emotions here: 'joy, sadness, anger, and fear.' Here, I would like you to consider that each emotion inherently gives us information; they are like informational packets; that provide crucial data about what is truly affecting us in negative ways. Fear is the emotion that arises if we feel threatened or shamed.

Sometimes you can experience a collision of anger, sadness, and fear, as these three tend to stick together and affect one another; whenever this happens, usually, one takes a predominant lead. Each emotion in this trio can be disempowering in and of itself or in concert with each other.

If you experience anxiety symptoms, it is important to know that it is not a character weakness or flaw; therefore, staying away from self-blame and shame is crucial as shame and blame can further exacerbate anxiety. Anxiety affects children, teens, and adults alike. The root cause of anxiety can be physical, psychological, or spiritual; thus, it's important to address the symptoms at the deep-subconscious levels in order to make substantial and meaningful changes.

Under the umbrella of anxiety, are a range of other disorders; these include but are not limited to separation anxiety disorder, selective mutism, specific phobia, social anxiety disorder, substance/medication-induced anxiety disorder, and anxiety disorder related to medical conditions. I give a brief overview of these so you can become aware of the symptoms.

What is anxiety

Anxiety is described as that feeling or emotion of unease, tension, worry, nervousness, fear, or dread. There are extreme expressions of anxiety; however, there are also normal levels of anxiety. Given a certain situation, anxiety may be a normal response. However, on the high extreme, when that state of tension, nervousness, and unease is constant and overwhelms us and interferes with our life and daily functioning, including normal duties and responsibilities of our work, and impairs relationships with others, then we need to manage the anxiety to get back into the normal range.

Signs & Symptoms of Anxiety

Feeling nervous, restless, or tense.

Having a sense of impending danger, panic, or doom.

Increased heart rate; heart racing or pounding.

Breathing rapidly (Hyperventilation).

Sweating.

Dry mouth.

Cold or sweaty hands.

Trembling.

Restlessness.

Feeling weak or tired.

Trouble concentrating or thinking about anything other than the present worry.

Difficulty sleeping.

Experiencing gastrointestinal (GI) problems.

Having difficulty controlling worry.

Having the urge to avoid things that trigger anxiety.

Types of Anxiety

Agoraphobia (ag-uh-ruh-FOE-be-uh)

It is a fear of enclosed places, e.g., inside a public bus or open places outside your house where you may feel trapped. It includes fear of crowded places with unfamiliar people. People with agoraphobia tend to stay mostly inside their homes to avoid elevated panic.

Generalized Anxiety Disorder (GAD)

Is persistent and excessive anxiety and worries over a six month period, where you experience at least three other symptoms. It includes restlessness or feeling keyed-up and on edge, experiencing muscle tension, irritability, sleep disturbance, difficulty concentrating (mind going blank), difficulty controlling, and worrying about activities or events constantly where the worry doesn't match up with the actual circumstance that you are or have been experiencing.

Panic attacks

It is often repeated episodes of abrupt, sudden, and spontaneous feelings of intense fear and anxiety. The intense uneasiness, fear, terror, or dread reaches its peak within minutes. You experience repeated thoughts or flashbacks of traumatic experiences with uncontrollable obsessive thoughts.

Often you might have a variety or combination of symptoms, e.g., feeling as if you are going crazy or fear of losing control, fear of dying, feeling dizzy, feelings of impending doom, shortness of breath, or feeling smothered, sweating or heat sensations or chills, chest pain, or a rapid heartbeat or pounding heart. Trembling or shaking, chest pain and nausea are some of the reasons panic attacks look a lot like heart attacks because of the symptoms-similarities. Some individuals may experience detachment from themselves (Derealization) or numbness or tingling sensations (Paresthesias).

It will be safer to get medical help if you are uncertain about distinguishing between a panic attack and a heart attack.

Social anxiety disorder (social phobia)

You avoid social situations because you experience intense levels of self-consciousness, thinking that others are perceiving you in a negative light and scrutinizing, judging, or ridiculing you, which leads you to act in ways that can result in embarrassment or humiliation. Such people tend to avoid social situations at all costs. Parents may see this in children or teenagers.

Specific phobias

Intense fear of a specific situation or object that you intentionally avoid, e.g., fear of flying, driving, and heights.

Substance-induced anxiety disorder

Misuse or abuse of drugs or withdrawal from them can lead to anxiety.

Medical conditions

Because we are body, soul, and spirit, we need to determine the root cause of the anxiety. Is there a physical reason for the emotions we are experiencing? Is it because of some unresolved trauma in our past? Is there a spiritual reason that you are experiencing elevated levels of anxiety?

There can be medical conditions that contribute to, cause or exacerbate anxiety. On the physical front, consideration has to be given to our endocrine system; for example, if our thyroid gland is not functioning optimally and thyroid hormones are elevated (Hyperthyroidism), one symptom of this medical-physical condition can look a lot like anxiety.

If thyroid hormones are low, on the other hand, a symptoms-cluster may resemble some aspects of depression.

For this reason, it is important to rule out any medical causes to treat the symptom of anxiety appropriately. If in a scenario like this one, where anxiety may be secondary to thyroid dysfunction, and you were treating your medical condition only with counseling or applying some spiritual remedial recourse, you may get some relief. But since the root cause is not addressed, you may continue to feel anxious, which worsens over time, erasing your self-esteem and confidence.

Other medical issues that can be associated with anxiety are:

Heart disease

Diabetes

Respiratory disorders, such as chronic obstructive pulmonary disease (COPD) and asthma

Drug misuse or withdrawal from anti-anxiety medication, alcohol

Irritable Bowel Syndrome (IBS).

Risk factors that contribute to Anxiety

Trauma:

Unresolved past childhood trauma can contribute to anxiety, or any traumatic events or situations can have the same effect and contribute to anxiety.

Stress

Our bodies are not created to hold elevated stress for extended periods. Sustained levels of stress can increase anxiety because it disrupts the normal biochemical balance in our bodies. If you are excessively worried about your health, relationships, finances, or a major event, you are setting yourself up for increased anxiety. Stress buildup can complicate other mental health and physical issues, which includes:

Drugs or alcohol

Misuse, abuse, or withdrawal can contribute to or exacerbate anxiety.

Heredity

There is a tendency that children might be prone to anxiety if one or both parents have it. However, heredity is not your destiny; even though you may have genes that make you susceptible, it still doesn't mean it is out of your control. Epigenetics is more powerful than genetics because you still have the power of choice. When you implement coping skills into your lifestyle and work through trauma materials, you can make a positive difference in managing your anxiety.

Complications of anxiety

If, however, you choose to allow your anxiety to run rampant without getting medical and/or psychological support (medication or counseling), anxiety can deteriorate into some of the following:

Depression (which often occurs with an anxiety disorder) or other mental health disorders.

Substance misuse

Trouble sleeping (insomnia).

Digestive or bowel problems, e.g., stomach pains, diarrhea, or constipation in irritable bowel syndrome (IBS)

Headaches and chronic pain

Social isolation

Problems functioning at school or work

Poor quality of life

Suicidal thoughts, intent, or plan.

What to do about it

Ask for help: There are available local counseling resources in communities that can cost you nothing to get the support you need, e.g., a local church, 'Celebrate Recovery' groups, and school counselors' offices are good places to start.

Find a supportive community: Join a group and participate in activities that you enjoy and that generally make you feel good. Social interactions and caring relationships can be an antidote to anxiety.

Learn coping skills to manage stress: Consider some of the strategies discussed later in this book.

Limit or avoid caffeine: As it can exacerbate anxiety symptoms.

Choose a healthy lifestyle: That includes a healthy diet, sleep, and some form of physical movement, including dancing, walking, or exercise.

Avoid alcohol or drug use: These can increase levels of anxiety. Seek support if you need help to avoid or quit.

How are anxiety disorders diagnosed?

There isn't a physical test to diagnose anxiety; however, once your physician rules out physical causes, they can refer you to counseling services, where a mental health clinician would assess your symptoms based on how they are interfering with your life before giving a diagnosis based on standard criteria for diagnoses.

Depression

Depression can be multifaceted; by that, I mean the extremes can range from numbness or an empty feeling to symptoms of irritability and significant cognitive changes to a decline in physical hygiene, including changes in weight or a slowing down or loss of spontaneous movement or sadness.

Sadness can be a normal response in the case of the loss of a loved one. In this case, the grief you experience, though normal, can lead to depression in the context of grieving. The sadness and grief in the face of loss are generally considered a temporary state but may still require you to get support to avoid remaining stuck in complicated grief.

You can overcome depression with appropriate help. It's not a flaw in your character or personality, nor is it something to feel ashamed about or keep hidden; otherwise, it can further isolate you from available help.

What is Depression?

Clinicians use a standard manual called the Diagnostic Statistical Manual (DSM) before diagnosing a client with clinical depression. A client exhibits at least five symptoms in the same 2-week period before a major depressive disorder (MDD) diagnosis is considered. Among the symptoms listed below, one has to be a decreased interest or pleasure in almost all activities. These symptoms must not be a co-occurring medical condition or drug abuse.

Other symptoms of Major Depressive Disorder (MDD) include:

Depressed mood (irritable mood for children)

Diminished interest or loss of pleasure

Weight changes or appetite disturbance

Sleep disturbance (Difficulty sleeping or excessive sleeping)

Fatigue or loss of energy

Feelings or worthlessness

Psychomotor agitation or retardation

Diminished ability to concentrate or think

Recurrent thoughts of death, recurrent suicidal ideation (or specific suicide plan or specific suicide attempt)

Types of Depression

There are nuances of depression that don't meet the standard criteria of clinical depression. However, each of these still takes a toll on our mental health. There are other types of depression. I will refer to a few, including:

Post-traumatic Stress Disorder (PTSD)

There are different levels of trauma that people experience, either real or threatened physical or sexual injury. Whether directly witnessing it occurring to others or vicariously experiencing it. It doesn't matter whether it is little 't' trauma or big 'T' trauma; the effect reaches deep into our souls and spirits.

Trauma is trauma. A teenager who may have been teased mercilessly in high school experiences trauma, or a veteran in an active war zone who has seen or done things that make it near impossible to return to normal civilian life without the invasive haunting of that trauma.

Trauma gets stuck at deep levels of our neuronal circuitry and needs to be dislodged and the negative charge reduced before you become free from its shackles.

However, for a PTSD diagnosis, at least one month must have passed since the traumatic event. Some symptoms will include:

Intrusive thoughts, including nightmares, flashbacks

Avoidance of thinking/talking about the traumatic event or of people, places, or activities

Negative changes in thinking and mood, e.g., difficulty recalling major details of the trauma, blaming oneself or others or the world, horror, or guilt. There is often a significant decrease in participation in significant activities, or feeling of detachment from others, or a persistent inability to have positive emotions.

Increased irritability, reckless behaviors, hypervigilance, problems with sleep or concentration, increased vigilance and arousal.

Persistent depressive disorder (Dysthymia)

This is a low-grade depression that lasts for about two years. Low grade because though some people experience symptoms of depression with an undercurrent of lack of joy, the symptoms are not as severe as major depressive disorder (MDD), and many can function in their daily lives.

Postpartum Depression

It occurs in women after childbirth. Sometimes it can be indistinguishable from a major depressive disorder. However, it can range from mild to severe. In mild symptoms, the mother can still care for the baby. In severe cases, the mother has difficulty caring for herself or her baby. Additionally, the risk of harming self and baby can be pronounced symptoms.

Seasonal Affective Disorder (SAD)

If you live in parts of the world where seasonal changes negatively affect your mood, primarily during the fall and/or winter months, and your mood improves during the spring and summer months, then SAD is a likely diagnosis. The key is that during the fall and winter months, the days are shorter, with less exposure to sunlight. As such, a person may experience symptoms of increased sleep (hypersomnia) or increased appetite, especially for comfort food.

Bipolar disorder

It has two extreme poles for your mood, cycling between highs and lows. The low period exhibits symptoms of depression, while the highs may involve excessive or frenetic energy, often tending to grandiosity, risky behaviors of pleasure-seeking, decreased need for sleep, and overspending. The high period is referred to as the manic stage of bipolar.

Psychotic depression

Some individuals experience depressive symptoms along with additional symptoms of believing in things that are not reality-based (delusions) or seeing or hearing things that other people neither see nor hear.

Complications of depression:

Chronic pain or illness

Self-harm

Suicide.

One leading cause of death in the United States is suicide, and depression contributes to this sad statistic. No age group is exempted. If you are living with depression, untreated or under-treated for depression, and have been thinking about suicide or have planned or attempted it, I want to let you know that you are not alone and that help to overcome depression is available to you. I have left resources that you can access.

What to do about it (Management strategies)

Lifestyle changes: including; sufficient restful sleep, diet, and exercise, are in your control, and implementing them can make a difference. Also, be intentional in adding fruits and vegetables to your dietary intake.

Naturopathic medicine: seek a licensed naturopathic physician who focuses on mental health to develop a client-specific treatment plan. The plan might include but is not limited to botanical medicine, acupuncture, homeopathy, or biofeedback.

Pharmacotherapy (pharmaceutical drugs/medications might be necessary)

Psychotherapy: there are a variety of therapeutic modalities to help individuals suffering from depression, including:

Cognitive Behavioral Therapy (CBT)

Interpersonal psychotherapy (IPT)

Problem-solving therapy (PST)

Self-Management/Self-Control Therapy

Stimulation techniques: these have also been approved by the FDA, including transcranial magnetic stimulation (TMS), especially for depression that is resistant to treatment; Electroconvulsive Therapy (ECT)[1]; Vagus Nerve Stimulation (VNS[2]

Trauma therapy modalities, including Eye Movement Desensitization Reprocessing **(EMDR)** or *Multichannel Eye Movement Integration (**MEMI**)*

Become informed: know your trigger signs for relapse so you can take the necessary steps to get the help you need.

The following are sites to provide additional and useful information:

National Institute of Mental Health: Depression

MedlinePlus: Depression

FamilyDoctor.org: Depression

Depression and Bipolar Support Alliance (DBSA)

---

1. https://my.clevelandclinic.org/health/treatments/9302-electroconvulsive-therapy
2. https://my.clevelandclinic.org/health/treatments/17598-vagus-nerve-stimulation

Families for Depression Awareness: Helpful websites specifically for late-onset depression include

MedlinePlus: Depression-elderly

National Institute of Mental Health: Older Adults: Depression and Suicide Facts

Alternatively, call 911 or the National Suicide Prevention Lifeline at 1-800-273-8255 (TYY: 1-800-799-4TTY (4889)).

Chapter 4 — Focused Visualization or Daydream

"As a man thinketh in his heart, so is he."

—Proverbs 23:7

"The only thing worse than being blind is having sight but no vision."

— Helen Keller

When we talk about visualization, we often confuse it with daydreaming. While the two concepts are similar, there is a distinguishing line between them that separates the two terms.

Daydreaming is more random, while visualization is a lot more intentional. Almost everyone can daydream. In daydreaming, you can let your mind wander without focusing on a particular object. Daydreaming can be a form of distraction and can get triggered without any external force influencing it.

Visualization, on the other hand, is a planned activity or practice. Visualization requires setting aside quiet time for the specific purpose of achieving a desired goal. Visualization is necessary for mental health. I almost think of visualization as a way we nourish our souls and build emotional resilience to manage stress, overcome trauma, and reduce anxiety or depression. It is like a mental exercise that we need to incorporate into our mental/emotional self-care routine.

To understand the concept of visualization, and to benefit from its practice, let us look at how the brain works and what we can learn from it.

Any understanding of our brain would describe it as a super complex circuitry of neurons that gets feedback from our physical senses. It is as a result of the firing of these neurons that our brain controls and regulates our physical life. It stores memory and manages our motor functioning. Many in the scientific field inform us that humans only use 10% of our brain's capacity and functionality. If that is true, then there is much more to learn and understand about this super-computer in our head because, at its very core, that's what the brain is a spectacular supercomputer.

Notwithstanding the scientific understanding of the brain, however, I want us to consider and conceptualize the brain as an efficient assistant, waiting for our commands. Our commands are the things we focus upon, think about, and verbalize. In other words, our brain receives commands to create our emotions or how we feel based on what we visualize and vocalize.

Our brain thinks in terms of pictures, and our eyes are the external part of our brain. The reason behind this is rather extraordinary. At the back of our eyeballs are the optic nerve, which connects directly to our brain. There is a special connection between our eyes and our brain. We have external sight and internal sight. Simply put, what we see influences how our brain functions, whether we see it outwardly as an object or inwardly as a thought.

Let us try a very simple exercise; go ahead and think about a person, place, or thing. Did you notice how readily you have an image or picture of that person, place, or thing? I gave verbal instruction, or in this case, you're reading black words on a white page, and you came up with a picture. The picture may represent pleasant memories or unpleasant ones, and they both are associated with corresponding emotions.

Memories comprise images, thoughts, and emotions. For example, a pleasant memory would evoke pleasant emotions; because of the associated thoughts and meaning attached to the memory. With a pleasant memory, you may also find yourself smiling and being pleased. An unpleasant memory, on the other hand, elicits a level of distress or uncomfortable feelings somewhere in your body and corresponds to the thoughts and meaning you have attached to the memory. Visualization is the key that makes the thoughts you are thinking real and vivid, resulting in the mood you experience. If that were all that the brain-eye connections does, then that would be enough. But there is more.

It can be said that our brain 'listens' to our thoughts and interprets the thought as a command to create a matching picture of that thought, which then translates into emotions or our moods. In other words, our thoughts become the foundational material that creates a corresponding mood state. What we think about and focus on, we eventually feel. Our thoughts are that powerful because it starts the cycle of producing our emotions or moods. And beyond that, when we vocalize our thoughts and repeat what we are thinking, it simply reinforces the mood and establishes that feedback loop.

In other words, our thoughts, whether positive or negative, are powerful commands that create mental or brain-derived pictures. And together with the things we say on a consistent basis, they become the material that cues up the brain to create an emotional state that matches the original instructions from what we visualize and speak. Simply put, when we have angry thoughts, we feel angry; when we have sad thoughts, we feel sad; when we have frightful thoughts, we feel fearful; when we have happy thoughts, we feel happy. You know that to be true because you have experienced it, even if you didn't make that connection before. The opposite is also true. A sad thought would never ever produce happy feelings or vice versa; angry or fearful thoughts can never produce feelings of empowerment. Having knowledge of how the brain works in this regard is liberating because then we can regulate our emotions by focusing on thoughts that create the emotions that empower us.

You might have heard it said, "Thoughts are things," and might be wondering what that statement means because what you know to be true is that thoughts are not tangible objects. However, what I want you to begin to understand nonetheless is that thoughts are solid things. It is almost as if they occupy a space in the grey matter in our brains. These thoughts or things we focus on can be measured in the way they cause our brain circuitry to respond. There are complex and complicated biochemical processes that occur in our brains and physical bodies that convert the thoughts we think and the words we speak into the emotions we feel, which are beyond the scope of this book.

Briefly, however, thoughts create the visual picture that directs the brain into producing and secreting bio-chemical substances into our bodies. The neurons in our brain secrete neurotransmitters, and the brain commands our endocrine glands to secrete hormones into our bodies. These biochemical substances closely match the thoughts that we focus on. The thoughts then show up as corresponding emotions we experience. I can't emphasize this point enough; if we can manage what we focus on or visualize, then we can control our mood state. As such, it is crucial that we monitor our thoughts and manage them so as to create empowering emotions that contribute to our well-being. Our responsibility also extends to challenging the type of negative thoughts that produces the feelings of being in the dumps.

The things we think about, focus on, meditate on or even worry about, and the things we verbalize are not incidental things. They are the material the brain uses to produce either empowering or disempowering moods or emotional experiences.

This is a key principle in what we know in psychology to be Cognitive Behavioral Therapy (CBT) in that there is a correlation between our thoughts and our emotions. When we embrace this principle and use it in our practical lives to regulate our emotions, we begin to understand the awesome responsibility and power we have at our disposal to use this key principle to our benefit. The truth is we all have this key. The sad fact is that we don't all use it to our benefit, but if we do, we would have the power to manage our moods by refocusing our thoughts. Therefore, it is crucially important to guide our thoughts in an intentional way and to redirect daydreaming in focused visualization so as to achieve an emotional state that empowers you.

When clients describe that they spontaneously feel overwhelmed, anxious, or even sad and promise me that they were not consciously thinking about something that will make them feel this way, I understand that an unconscious thought-pattern has been established in their lives. It's like a 'neuronal' super-highway has been created and can be easily triggered to create or produce emotions along that pathway in super-fast ways.

In order to adjust our emotions to ones that are more empowering, we need to replace them with positive thoughts that would elicit those supportive emotions, and here is where visualization is at its best and shines.

A practical strategy you can implement in your daily life is to create a mental place in your mind where you feel loved, joyous, and peaceful, a place where you experience feelings of being centered and grounded. Some clients describe it as their "happy place."

In creating this place, I invite you to think of a beautiful or happy place that you have either visited or would like to visit, and if this does not come readily to you, then we can create such a place using our internal eye to visualize such a place where you believe you will feel refreshed and restored. A quick internet search can stimulate picturesque beauty that is just a couple of clicks away. I invite my clients to punctuate their day with this focused visualization by simply thinking of this place that makes them feel emotionally supported. The simple fact of focused visualization is that it will set in motion the creation of good and positive emotions. What is even more astonishing is that all this is done simply with the right kind of thoughts.

In this place, visualize yourself in the picture. Are you walking along a shoreline barefoot with your sandals in your hand? Are you sitting on a park bench? Are you lying on a towel, looking up at the evening sky with all the hues of pink and orange? Is it a cloudless sky? Or does it have those bulky clouds that look like large animals sometimes, or perhaps there are those thin strewn clouds that look like lace? Go all out to make this place exquisitely yours. Use as many of the five senses as you can to bring this place to life. Describe all the things you see in this picture and their colors with different shades and hues. Are there trees or rocks, mountains, waterfalls, oceans, and sunsets on the horizon? Describe them all in as vivid detail that your imagination can muster. Are there birds or butterflies in your picture? If you want them, then simply 'put' them in. Then see them with your inner eye; because when you 'see' them, the brain interprets the thought-commands as if you are there with all the positive feelings that the visual image elicits. The more descriptors you use, in the creation of your 'happy place,' the more you fine-tunes the image.

When you are finished with the internal sight (visualization), then bring to life what you hear, are there sounds in this place? Do you hear birds chirping or seagulls squawking? Do you hear the waves crashing or water rushing over rocks in a stream nearby or in the distance? After you are satisfied with the sounds you created, turn your attention to what you feel on your skin. Is it a hot day, a warm or muggy one, or are you feeling a cool breeze? Is the temperature just the way you like it? This place is perfect for you. It makes you relaxed, and you feel good being there.

The beauty of creating this place is that you may add anything to your picture that continues to improve your mood, or you may remove things you don't like. It is allowed because you are making it uniquely your happy place.

After you would have created your place to your satisfaction, then I invite you to describe how you feel being in such a place. I can tell you with 100% certainty it would be a good feeling. You may even notice a smile on your face as you describe your happy place. And without realizing it, you have brought into reality an experience that you are having in the present, and in the now, even though you are not physically in that place, you elicit the emotions as if you were there physically. You have visualized something that brought you joy and emotional nourishment.

I often invite clients to come up with a word or phrase that describes how they feel when they think of themselves in that place and insert that word somewhere into that picture. This word can be placed in the skies, somewhere in the clouds, right in front of you, or on the horizon.

Allow that word to have a definition by giving it a distinct font, color, and size. An example would be that the word is in large, bold blue, and solid font, or perhaps you like the thin cursive style. All that matters is that you like it. This chosen word needs to be in the picture each time you think/visualize that happy place or scene so that eventually, by simply thinking of that word, the positive feelings or emotions are also evoked, and in time after you have paired the word or phrase with your unique happy place, you will find that when you think of the word you will experience good, happy feelings. Now that is the beauty of visualization. Also, there is no limit to the happy places you can create. Have fun and create as many as your heart desires.

If you have difficulty coming up with an innovative imaginary scene; then focus on your current environment and using as many of your five senses as possible, describe what you are seeing, identify the sounds they are hearing, listen intently and tune in well; you may come up with more than one sound; then let your nose take the lead to fragrances you are smelling. If there is no outstanding fragrance in the environment, then arbitrarily include some preferred fragrance, example, a special candle, you get to choose and add variety to this happy place, and when you are satisfied, focus on the seat you're resting on, and describe how it holds up your body. The singular goal is to give your mind the material to create a happy mood state. If there is an iota of enjoyment during the activity, then you are on the right track. If you do not like the activity, then replace it with something else that you enjoy.

Another visualization exercise I teach and guide my clients through is concretizing the area of distress in their lives. For example, if you tend to feel anxious "*for no reason*" throughout your day, then impose a shape onto the anxiety. What shape would you give it? Make it up. Is it a square or a circle, or perhaps a blob? Do you feel more comfortable with a hexagon or a knotted rope? It doesn't matter. Arbitrarily, give it a shape.

If it had a size, would it be small, medium, or large? If the anxiety had a color, then what color would you see it in, and if it had a temperature, would it be cold or hot? You may also give the object a texture; is it rough, callous, or smooth?

After you would have concretized the anxiety or distress, then find its location in your body. Where in your body do you feel tense when you are anxious, angry, or fearful? For example, do you feel as if there is a knot in your belly? or a lump in your throat? Does your jaw automatically clench? Does a shiver run down your entire body?

Each one of us has a signature physical response to elevated emotions and locating the stagnated emotion in your body is helpful. I then guide clients to use their internal mind's eye to substitute this object in the place where they feel the sensation in their body. Now here is where visualization can be fun. You get to imagine and think of ways to reduce the distressing object to a size that is manageable. I often like to think of a healing light encapsulating the noxious object while simultaneously disintegrating it into smaller pieces so that it loses its consolidating or terrorizing power that causes you distress and dis-ease in your body; you may allow the concretized object to evaporate or to leave your body in a way that you feel more in control.

It is different for many people, but in the end, these visualization skills and techniques use the way the brain works to keep us emotionally healthy and whole.

Practicing visualization as a part of our daily routine is the way we care for our souls. Emotional awareness and emotional self-care are necessary elements for our mental health and well-being.

Using mental brain activities like those described above helps build emotional resilience to fill or replenish our emotional reservoir in a way that when the ups and downs, twists, and sudden turns occur in our lives, we would have enough in our emotional bank when a major emotional withdrawal is made.

Chapter 5 — Emotional Awareness

"Jesus grew in wisdom and in stature and in favor with God and all the people."

— Luke 2:52 NLT

"So don't bother correcting mockers; they will only hate you. But correct the wise, and they will love you."

— Proverbs 9:8 NLT

I start this chapter with the end in mind that emotional awareness is a necessity and not an option. We need to be emotionally aware in order to thrive, flourish, prosper, and live wholesome lives. To be aware of the emotional tumult and flux that occurs inside of us is to be in touch with the most vulnerable parts of ourselves. To protect that vulnerable part of our being, some people erect rigid emotional defenses that give a false veneer of safety and security. Often, we rationalize and justify the reasons for our behavior, or worse yet, we simply deny our vulnerability to deflect from the sensitized, hurting parts of our soul. It is not uncommon for some individuals to be unaware of the powerful emotional undercurrent that keeps them unsettled with constant deep agitation and dis-ease, which permeates every aspect of their lives. The quiet storm raging on the inside of us continues to wreak havoc in our bodies, in our souls, and in our spirits, with each passing day showing up as physical illness, mental stress, and emotional breakdowns. In the times that we live in and the lives that we lead, it's very easy to get lost and lose contact with the plumbline of our authentic emotional states. Often, instead of acknowledging, validating, and giving language to our emotions, we tend to seek out any panacea or multiple distractions to dull the deep and dreadful emotional pain.

Emotional awareness is an essential and foundational aspect of our mental and emotional health and well-being. It is to our hazard if we are emotionally unaware. If numbness or neglect of our emotions continue, we will be trading off our emotional well-being for constant unrest and agitation at deep levels of our being. A lack of emotional awareness allows feelings of shame, guilt, anger, fear, sadness, self-hatred, resentment, and more of its kind to fester as a distinctive rot that invariably becomes corrosive to our relationships with ourselves and others.

And when we consistently react in negative putrid ways, it pushes the people we love away from us and ultimately makes us feel even more hurt, disconnected and isolated than we were before.

A lack of emotional awareness not only causes an individual to lose touch with the most vulnerable part of themselves but also makes them feel disconnected and lost. No matter how hard they try to get rid of the unsettling anguish in their stunted emotional soul, they find themselves trapped in the same vicious vortex.

The challenge is that some people aren't even aware that they are unaware of their emotional ineptitude and numbness. We don't know what we don't know. We have these blinders on that make us think that the way we see a thing is the truth about that thing. And we deceive ourselves. To become emotionally aware is to notice the patterns in your life and relationships, whether those relationships are at work, at home, or among friends, acquaintances, roommates or loved ones. You begin to notice that the same issues keep re-occurring in different scenarios. It is as if you attract a specific type of dysfunction. Wherever you go, and no matter how long you stay and even with a different cast of characters, you encounter the same unresolved emotional issue.

This is a flashing neon sign that the problem must, of course, lie with you. The initial realization is a painful one to reckon with. We would rather accuse, blame or shame others because doing so temporarily soothes the emotional anguish. No matter how long you've anticipated the conclusion that you are the problem, the moment that you realize it for the first time is always one of extreme pain. It is important to reflect on that moment and realize that the way you reacted was perhaps a result of some unhealed emotional issue. Unhealed trauma tends to resurface with a rhythmic pulse of intrusion when we face a similar or threatening situation that reminds us of the unhealed wound.

The tyranny of an unhealed wound is an equal opportunity abuser. No one escapes its long tentacled arm that keeps us stuck. It doesn't even matter how many commas and zeros are in your bank account; it cannot provide emotional integrity because our emotional well-being is pivoted on emotional awareness.

The beauty of emotional awareness is that it is not dependent on being rich or poor, black, brown, yellow, white or tanned; it has nothing to do with your status in life, or lack of it. It is simply available to all who work at growing in their emotional stature.

With all that said, this chapter revolves around emotional awareness and how a pivotal recognition and understanding of one's own emotions is to our well-being.

I have developed an emotional awareness exercise to help the reader do a deep dive into the unresolved emotional material submerged in the subconscious. It is simply about identifying, acknowledging, and giving voice to these unspoken emotions. If you are not one of my former clients, it would be for you the very first time doing an exercise like this. But I invite you into this intentional journey of emotional awareness to neutralize the devastating effect that these unresolved emotions have on your emotional health.

Let me paint a word picture to help you conceptualize the emotional work you are about to embark on. Think of an iceberg in the ocean. This made you see a large block of ice floating on top of the ocean. What you don't see but intuitively know is there is a huge block of ice below the water's surface. It is said that 1/3 of the iceberg is above sea level and 2/3 beneath sea level. If the iceberg we see above is massive, then the iceberg beneath the surface, which we do not see, is twice as massive in depth and size. It is twice as deep and twice as wide compared to what we see on the surface. The depth of the iceberg is submerged and hidden, just like your unresolved emotional woundedness and pain are submerged and hidden. The part of the iceberg that we see above sea level can be compared to the symptoms or behavior others can recognize. Your childhood traumas, the emotional neglect or depravity that suffocated your soul lies deep within you. It takes all those years and sometimes decades to layer deposits into the depths of your being, siphoning and leaking out the integrity of emotional wholeness. But becoming emotionally aware is like plumbing the depths to dive deep to understand the scope of impact. Because the moment we see the extent of the submerged material and give it language, it loses its unrelenting grip on our lives.

With that in mind, let us begin the "Emotional Awareness" (EA) exercise. You may have to read through the seven steps first, so you will know what each step entails.

The exercise is simple yet profound for the reasons I explained above:

Step 1: Quiet Place

Find a quiet place and take a pen, a sheet of paper, and a timer instrument with you (for example, a watch or phone). This is a place where no one is going to disturb you. Make sure it's also a time that you do not have any personal responsibilities or duties that would distract you from focusing during the exercise. If you are using your phone, use only the timing feature so no incoming calls can derail you.

Step 2: Sit Comfortably

Sit down on the ground or on a flat surface and make sure you're comfortable.

Step 3: Set Timer

Once you are seated comfortably, set the timer for a maximum of six (6) minutes.

Step 4: Recall

Bring to mind a disturbing memory. It can be the worst memory for you or one that comes up for you often. Imagine yourself in that memory. (It is often the younger version of yourself).

Step 5: Image of Younger Self

Focus on the younger version of yourself, and ask: "what was I feeling?" The key is your feelings. Keep your focus on what you were feeling, not what you were thinking at that time.

Step 6: Give Voice to Your Emotions

Write descriptive, emotional words about what you were feeling on the sheet of paper, and as you write the words down, simultaneously verbalize the words just loud enough so that your ears can hear the resonance of your own voice.

For example, if you felt anxious, lonely, sad, angry, fearful, confused, abandoned, rejected, not good enough, not loved, shame, guilt, or any other emotions that disturbed you, then say it out loud and write it down. By saying it out loud, your ears will hear the resonance of your voice as you acknowledge the emotions, which in turn gives definition and form to the emotions that were beforehand an ambiguous and nebulous terror. Saying the descriptive, emotional words (or phrases) out loud also makes you aware of your emotions, which is the first step in your emotional awareness journey. If other memories bubble up and come in front of your mind, think of them as friends from the past re-introducing themselves to you; welcome that new memory with the same question: "What was I feeling?" and continue to write the emotional words down until the timer alarm goes off.

Step 7: Hands Resting on Body

When the timer goes off, look at what you wrote down on your sheet of paper and simultaneously place your hands on the area of your body that generally feels tense when you get triggered; for example, if your chest generally gets tight and you breathe shallowly, then place your hands on your chest. If it is your belly that feels 'wonky,' place your hands there. If it is your jaws that get tight, then gently place both your hands on your jaw, cradling them, and then validate your emotions with five self-soothing statements, where you speak to yourself in the 3rd person. I am using my first name as an example:

Carolyn, these emotions are appropriate given the circumstances

Carolyn, these emotions are valid

Carolyn, you did the best you could.

Carolyn, I'm super proud of you.

Carolyn, I love you

The intention of addressing yourself in the third person is to set it up where your present adult self is speaking to the younger version of yourself so that part of yourself feels seen and heard.

Perhaps the most important thing is to recognize and understand that these hidden emotions have the strongest influence on your life's perspective. Hence placing your gentle attention on them can change the very structure of the memory.

The recommendation is that you complete this exercise at least once daily. You may start with another disturbing memory or remain with the same one but keep exploring the memory as different facets of that past experience may be revealed as you continue to do the deep dive. When you ask yourself, "what was I feeling?" it invites other emotions to introduce themselves to you.

Developing your emotional awareness adds the values of integrity and authenticity to your soul's well-being, allowing you to build resiliency and reduce the charge of the negative emotional undercurrent.

Chapter 6 — Right Thoughts and Right Words: the Master Key

"Whether you think you can or you think you can't — you're right."

— Henry Ford

"Fix your thoughts on what is true, honorable, right, pure, lovely, and admirable. Think about things that are excellent and worthy of praise."

— Philippians 4: 8 NLT

A physical key conjures up the understanding of an emblem that opens up barriers — barriers such as doors and gates. We have keys for several doors: postal boxes, car doors, and our homes. We also have electronic keys and passwords that protect valuable, personal, and sensitive information and beyond that, there is now talk about using fingerprints and eye scans to let you in where you won't ordinarily be admitted without this biological type of key.

Keys are ubiquitous; you find them everywhere. I would hazard a guess that every adult has at least one key in his or her possession at any one time. We intuitively know that if a key doesn't fit into a keyhole of the door, then it is not the emblem that unlocks that door. Thus, we have to try another key. And only the right key unlocks that particular door. The same can be said of a 'key principle.' A key principle opens up opportunities, insights, and understanding, much like the right key opens up a door; a key principle opens up solutions that can benefit our lives.

Having said all that, I want to introduce a master key or a principle for life, and the intention is that it helps you achieve and maintain your mental health.

Thoughts and words are the key that creates and influences our mental health. However, it is the right kind of thoughts and the right kind of words that have the power to influence your life and relationships.

Many do not generally know the power of the right thoughts and words. Thoughts and words impact our relationships and worldview perspective. Another way to describe this is by saying what you think about you will eventually believe, and what you believe you will eventually speak; and when you speak what you believe, you create either life or death into your relationships and reality.

The ancient king Solomon was said to be the wisest man of his time. His instructions ring true even today when he says,

"He, who guards his mouth and his tongue, keeps himself from calamity." —Proverbs 21:23 (NIV)

The task, then, is to know how to manage our thinking and to speak in purposeful and intentional ways so that we can achieve mental and emotional health. It is as simple as that and yet neglected by many. It is truly sad when people allow their minds to wander randomly and carelessly, entertaining any thoughts that spring up. Minding your mind is a good adage to reflect upon at this point. We have to be diligent in assessing what we ponder or focus our attention on. We must think about what we think about and how we think and challenge negative or disempowering thoughts. Because as described in earlier chapters, our thoughts are solid things that take up space in our brain, which then attracts other corresponding emotions. So the master key is 'right thoughts and right words.'

Think the thoughts and speak the words that create the wholesome life that at this time escapes you. Think right, true, honorable thoughts that will empower and benefit you and are in your best interest. You become what you think, and you create what you speak. Your thoughts and words are powerful in that they create your reality; and have the untapped potential to unlock many good opportunities before us, opportunities that might take us to a higher level of insight and a stable perspective of our life. You get more of what you focus on. If you think about, focus on, or worry about things that are out of control, more situations of the same kind will be attracted into your sphere. You will get more of the negative stuff being attracted to your experience.

Thinking in and of itself must not be considered good or bad. However, a certain thought pattern often opens up associated or matching emotions. Negative thoughts will fill us with emotions that keep us in a negative head and heart space. We feel the negativity in our bodies. You won't presume a key good if it opens up a beautifully decorated room. The same is true for the key that unlocks a room filled with cold darkness and void. The key itself is not bad. The parallel is that the act of thinking and speaking is neither good nor bad. It is the type of thoughts we give attention to and focus or ponder upon that becomes the determining factor. As such, the 'right thoughts and right words' combined become the key to attaining mental health

Our thoughts and our words work in unison like two peas in the same pod. I reflect on two ancient texts that say it better than I ever could: "For the mouth speaks what the heart is full of" (Matthew 12:34; Luke 6:45), and there is a caution in the other text, which says, "Above all else, guard your heart, for it is the wellspring of life." (Proverbs 4:23)

In my acupuncture training, I learned that the heart and the tongue are connected. Whether we ponder a silent thought in our hearts or voice that thought in the things we say on a consistent basis, the effect is the same; it eventually creates our reality.

The truth is that an individual can choose good, uplifting, and empowering thoughts to focus on or choose another set of thoughts that disempowers, discourages, angers, and generally disheartens them.

We must re-learn how to think and structure our thoughts in a way that unlocks and gives us access to the emotional health and stability available to us.

We eventually create a reality that mirrors and reflects our thoughts and words. Our thoughts become and act like a lens, and it is through these lenses that we perceive the world. The reason I'm emphasizing the point is that every single person has the ability to re-create their internal environment by grasping this truth and re-training themselves to have thoughts and words that benefit them. Our external environment is a mirror of our internal environment. This is not some kind of psychobabble; this is the key to launching you into a place to achieve and maintain your mental health.

Thoughts and words have a magnetic charge.

We've all had those experiences of regurgitating a situation that upsets or angers us and when we find ourselves thinking, murmuring, grumbling, and complaining about those things, what seems to follow are a series of events or situations that continue to exacerbate that initial upset feeling. These series of events aggravating the situation are not coincidental. This is because 'Like begets like.' The magnetic field attracts and binds materials that resonate with it.

Playing with magnets reinforces the point. On the attraction side, you can feel the invisible pull of two magnets. Within a certain range, the force pulls and snaps another magnet. You may also find that a silver nail clip can clasp onto the magnet as well, even though the nail clip doesn't have any magnetic ability in and of itself, but because there is metal in the silver nail clip, it is the metal that resonates and binds with the magnet.

You will also notice that the magnet has no power to hold and attract anything that doesn't have the material the magnet is made from, such as a pencil or a plastic pen, or paper; these materials don't clasp onto a magnet; because these materials are of a different kind. The point I'm making here is that the magnetic ability of your thoughts and words is the key you can apply to change your emotions. And the way you do this is to challenge negative thoughts or reframe and select an alternative meaning to the distressing situation you are experiencing. Left unchallenged, the disempowering emotions attract other situations into your life that maintain the initial distressing emotions.

Alcoholics Anonymous (AA) has a famous mantra that is applicable here "Nothing Changes if Nothing Changes." In other words, if you change one pattern of thinking and verbalizing, then you have made a substantial change in the overall pattern of your mental health. Albert Einstein says it another way; "The definition of insanity is doing the same thing over and over again and expecting a different result."

Achieving wholeness in your mental health requires an intentional change in your thoughts and words. Alternatively, if you do not make a simple change, you will keep doing what you have always done, and consequently, you will get what you have always gotten — a stalemate where your mental health is concerned.

When you seek out and choose an alternative meaning to a perceived negative situation you are encountering, it changes your perspective and the things that you look at can and will change. How we respond to things, people, and places will change.

One individual may see a glass as half-full, while the other sees that same glass as half-empty. The perspective of each person influences and affects their emotional response to the same object or situation. Each perspective has a certain emotion that is attached to that perspective. The individual who says that the glass is half full has a perspective of abundant supply and thoughts of gratitude, while the one who sees the glass as half-empty has an emotional perspective of lack, deficit, and insufficiency.

In the next chapter, I reinforced the importance of having an emotional self-care routine. It is in this routine you self-reflect upon and examine your perspective or patterns of thinking. When you intentionally engage in purposeful thinking and self-reflection, you will notice your own thought patterns and reactions. By doing this analysis, you identify your unique perspective on how you view your life events or personal situations and the meaning you have affixed to those things or situations.

Often internal distress arises when you think that something is awful. Once you label any situation, person, thing, emotion, or feeling as bad, the meaning of bad invariably takes on the magnetism that the word brings. This later initiates a cascade of similar situations, persons, things, emotions, or feelings into your emotional-magnetic orbit, bringing more of its kinds because like attracts like. Sooner than later, the cluster of these emotions increases the enormity of an emotional tornado, where you will be at the mercy of its punishing force of negativity and chaos. Conversely, the opposite is true; if we were to find an alternative meaning and reframe the facts of a negative situation into an opposite positive or more useful thought or meaning, then the key shall still work, only this time it attracts situations, persons, things, emotions or feelings that have resonance with your positive magnetism; and often you find yourself attracting solutions, opportunities, and insights, which generally leaves you with an improved mood.

Practically speaking, here's what a simple change in your words might sound like, instead of saying something is bad and getting angry or sad over it, try saying instead, "it is what it is, and I will be okay, and this too shall pass, or something good can come out of this" by this simple change in your language and perspective you set in motion a magnetic field that attracts other thoughts and emotions that resonates and matches with the core thoughts. Thus, you would be more inclined to feel uplifted and restored instead of feeling stressed or tense.

Challenging one's negative thoughts requires immense patience. When we have one negative thought or meaning about a certain thing or event, we should go a step further to replace that negative thought with an opposite and positive thought so that the negative thought does not go unchallenged. If an unopposed negative thought has its free sway in one's life, it will only deposit what it consists of, namely the sad, depressed or angry feelings in your body. And just like a dark cloud that showers us with heavy rainfall, the unopposed negative thought will throttle you for longer than you can imagine, sometimes hours, days, weeks, months, years, or even decades, with mental distress, anxiety, or depression. An unexamined thought controls and even manipulates our emotions each time it hovers over us, not unlike a puppeteer who manipulates a puppet.

The choice to do the work is a noble one. We must consistently choose the right thoughts and right words. It is the task we have to engage in to achieve and maintain mental health.

Chapter 7 — Emotional Self-Care Routine

When we think of self-care, our minds generally go to the physical hygiene type of self-care. We have unique and different morning hygiene routines. This routine consisting of several steps varies from person to person; we shower, brush our teeth, comb our hair, put on creams, lotions, oils, and perfumes, and polish our physical body, to meet the day and interact in public. This routine is crucial because we want to be presentable before the world. Otherwise, we would feel self-conscious and insecure if people considered us dirty or disheveled in any way.

Let us consider the habitual things of our morning routines; in today's modern world, some people reach for their cell phones on their nightstands as soon as they open their eyes. Some may whisper a prayer of gratitude to live another day; some may sit straight up and head to the kitchen to brew the first-morning coffee, while others may head straight to the bathroom to brush their teeth, look in the mirror, and wash their face. Whatever the order of our morning routines, it is usually consistent with the same daily tasks we chose. Even when a morning routine is different for different people living in the same house, there is a consistent way that individuals implement their morning routine. The point I'm making is that we all have morning routines or established patterns of what we choose to do each morning after waking up. In the same manner, we need to adopt an emotional self-care routine.

Here is the parallel; emotional self-care is as important as physical self-care and spiritual self-care. It is not that one is more important than the others, but they are all necessary for a person's well-being. Emotional self-care is often done alone in a serene and quiet place so that we can self-reflect. However, it is important to know that emotional self-care also requires a routine. This routine is essential to maintain a positive structure in our life 's experience.

The ever-demanding world puts an enormous amount of pressure and stress on our psyche. Building up our emotional resources is extremely important to deal with this pressure, or else we would be constantly taxed and emotionally maxed-out. Emotional health needs a level of care and intention to make it a habit and routine.

We need to have a routine that helps us to take care of our mental and emotional health. Contrary to popular beliefs, emotional self-care should be an ingrained practice. Do not buy into the lie that self-care is selfish. It is not! It is an expression of love towards yourself, and before you can love or take care of anybody else, you need to first love and care for your own self. Below I offer some ideas regarding how you may care for yourself emotionally. Most may cost you nothing financially, while some may require you to pay for human connection and emotional support.

Let us begin with a simple question:

What is emotional self-care?

It includes intentionally spending quiet, reflective time examining our thoughts and making decisions during those times on how we would purposefully direct our lives by adjusting, course-correcting, or replacing the negative, dysfunctional thinking. The thoughts we focus on and the way we conceptualize our responsibility to ourselves, and other significant relationships are crucial for your well-being.

Upon hearing the word, 'self-care,' many people perceive it as 'me-time'; truth be told, this is not entirely wrong. Even though this is true, emotional self-care is also about nourishing and caring for your feelings. When you nurture and process your feelings frequently, you will have the power to calm your nervous system — this will significantly decrease stress. Emotional self-care requires slow, still, dedicated time and a quiet place with a focused, intentional goal. Emotional self-care is not a group project or a social event; it is mostly done in solitude and silence. The fact of being with oneself and with one's thoughts without the compulsion or the tyranny of a "things to do list" opens up space to focus on the sensitive, soft, and pliable parts of your being. It also grants you the beauty of being mindful of the sights and sounds around you.

Your Breath

Observing your breath is one of the best places to start your emotional self-care routine. Your breath can help you emotionally regulate in a way other things might not.

Anxiety shows up in your breath first. When you are anxious, you will notice your breath turn shallow and rapid. Conversely, the opposite is also true; if you deliberately start breathing shallowly or rapidly, you will begin to experience symptoms of anxiety. It is the change in your breath that reflects the change in your emotions.

When you slow down your breathing, it relieves the hovering or overwhelming anxiety. It induces a calming effect on your body. However, the effort must be intentional. Focusing on how your belly goes in and out begins to center and ground you. Then try to breathe slower, focusing solely on your breathing until you start feeling relaxed. A slow breath can help to stimulate the parasympathetic nervous system (The rest and digest system) — this is the nervous system we want to operate from most of the time. By doing so, we build up our emotional resources.

Consider the '4-7-8' parasympathetic breathing technique, and punctuate your day with its frequent use. Keep your eyes closed and breathe in while counting slowly till 4, and hold that inhaled breath for the count of 7 and exhale through your mouth at the count of 8. Repeat at least three times or as many times until you feel your body relaxing.

You may also consider trying any preferred meditation apps. Today's market is flooded with excellent meditation apps offering you a variety to choose from.

Surround Yourself with Nature

Nature is one of the greatest relievers, bar none. Nature provides tranquility and peace to substitute and replace strain, tension, or stress. Such is the power of being in and surrounding yourself with nature.

Choosing parts of nature where you have a panoramic or wide expansive view of large bodies of water, like the ocean or lakes where the horizons meet with the sun at sunset; or exposing oneself to witness a sunrise or walking through a hiking trail with trees or flowers, birds or, butterflies and the like regulates our nervous system like no other.

'***Panoramic nature views***' have a special significance and are almost in a category all by themselves. When we see grandeur and majesty, it powerfully informs us of our finiteness. Though our problems seem big, threatening, and impossible at the time, they are still smaller than the expanse of what we are a part of.

Another quick grounding tip would be to lean against a tree, with the full length of your spine being supported by the tree — this can give you a sense that you're not alone in this world. While leaning against a tree, focus on taking deep breaths. Alternatively, you may simply sit under a tree or among the flowers while practicing the visualization techniques shared in the previous chapter or the 5 senses mindfulness I'm about to share.

Five Senses Mindfulness

Focus on the environment where you are and utilize your physical senses of sight, sound, smell, taste, and touch as much as you can, as many as you can at a time. What do you see? Identify the objects in the room or in nature, or you can identify them; you may also look for objects in a preferred color; for example, how many objects in orange can you identify? How many colors can you identify; what do you hear? Do you recognize any distinct sounds? You will have to tune in and practice the sense of sound until you recognize the sound of silence around you. Does any fragrance or odor awaken your sense of smell? Allow yourself to experiment with the environment; for example, if there are no specific fragrances, then you can arbitrarily incorporate one by adding a favorite Essential Oils (EO). A lot of people like 'Lavender,' as it has a special quality to help relax you. But you may try a variety of Essential oils that make your heart smile. You may whiff the fragrance from the bottle, or you may shake the bottle to your fingertip and apply it around your nostrils. Since Essential oils are concentrated, they can irritate your skin. To alleviate that irritation, you may add a drop or two of the Essential oil to a drop of carrier oil, for example, olive oil or castor oil, before applying it to your skin.

The sense of taste may require a bit of innovation. If you are doing this exercise and you don't have a snack at hand, then try pressing the tip of your tongue onto the roof of your mouth and holding it for a few seconds. Alternatively, you may run your tongue around the inside of your teeth and then on the outside of your teeth with your mouth closed, all the while focusing on the change of texture of your palate or teeth and tasting your breath. If, on the other hand, you do have a snack, then take 'ant-size' bites and notice how it feels on your tongue, and observe whether it produces little or much saliva.

After that, shift your attention; can you feel the ground where you are sitting or lying down?

What do you feel?

Asking yourself and reflecting upon such questions can give you a sense of being grounded and present with yourself. It also recalibrates and keeps you grounded and in your body.

The present is all you have. Your physical body is right here. It is not there in the past, nor are you physically in the future; you will always be here; so notice the moment, so you can enjoy it.

The Emotional Awareness Exercise

We spoke about the importance of being emotionally aware in a previous chapter. As such, this exercise can be done during your emotional self-care routine.

Develop A Planned Future Response

While we have no power over our future and can't control the upcoming events, and more importantly, while we have no control over how another human being responds to us, we do have power over our reactions to those events. You have the power to take a deep breath, treat yourself with kindness, and discover methods to be optimistic and calm. Instead of bursting out in anger, or being paralyzed with anxiety, you can visualize how you would prefer to respond. And you could do this ahead of time during a visualization exercise in your emotional self-care routine. The purpose of this is to help you feel prepared so that when a similar or actual situation occurs, you can replicate what you visualize.

Here is how you develop planned future responses:

Mentally Rehearse and Reinforcing Healthy Boundaries

Healthy boundaries can protect you and help you build auto-emotional responses. Boundaries teach you to say 'Yes' and 'No' where necessary. Once you are aware of certain individuals and settings that trigger an angry response and steal calm and serenity from you, you have the choice to not be around these individuals. Decline all the invitations to be constantly around your stressors. It is important to protect your heart space. This may even be necessary for individuals who share your DNA. You can always communicate your boundaries to friends and families. Because you have control over your choices — always remember you can control how you respond.

Develop Your Tribe of Support

Everybody needs good and positive friends. We all need a minimum of one good and positive friend in our life. We can also have two but limit to three good and positive friends because we often do not have the emotional energy for more than that. Everything and anything that is important needs intentional effort; it requires work, needs, nourishment, and nurture to improve it. The same goes for friendships. Good friendships require work to cause them to grow, develop, and be sustained. Seek quality in a few relationships rather than quantity.

Sit with your good friends and family regularly. Being physically present with other people has become extremely crucial in a society that depends on social media. Spend time with people who will make you laugh and listen to you when you need to talk. When you're out with friends, put your phone away and make it a habit to be present and fully attentive. You will see the gradual change with this practice in your relationship — and you'd be able to live in the moment and learn to cherish it. This will leave little room for regrets in the future.

Verbalize Gratitude

If there are a zillion things going wrong in your life and relationships, you need to look ever more closely; to discover one thing or a fraction of a thing that is going right. Focus on that fraction or that singular thing going right and whisper, "I am grateful."

Keep a thankfulness journal where you list several items each day for which you are grateful has helped many people turn their ingratitude into the virtue of gratitude. Additionally, daily expression of gratitude is beneficial. It will improve your mood. When someone does anything small for you, verbalize your gratitude — consider sending notes, or crafting a text-message or leaving a voice message to people expressing your gratitude that they are in your life.

Journaling

Journals are a blessing for those who find them useful; you can keep a record of how you feel at a single point in time. It is a great way to connect with yourself. You can easily reflect and become aware of your emotions by journaling. It does not necessarily have to be a big book; a small pocket journal will work just as well since you can take it with you. I often invite clients to write their stories. We all have a story and should become familiar with it. It is a way to allow movement from the stagnant emotions that reside in our bodies. It validates the experience with words and language. This is an important step in our healing journey.

Other Recommendations

Acknowledge your progress — No matter how little your progress is, when you encourage yourself and nurture your progress, it grows. It needs small, incremental steps before your progress becomes big and bold. A balanced view of celebrating one's progress is to focus on your growth, and soon, you will build momentum in the right direction. Your emotional and physical health are intertwined. Sound physical health often translates to a healthy emotional self. Use these simple tips for your physical health.

Your body is meant to move, so exercise frequently. A brisk walk on a cool afternoon or dancing to your favorite jam, as if no one's watching or spring cleaning your home, condo, or apartment, all count as exercise because you're moving your body.

Consider decreasing caffeine and soda intake, as these can exacerbate anxiety.

Sleep! The cycle of work and rest is necessary for healthy functioning. There is hardly any substitute for a good night's uninterrupted sleep and waking up refreshed. Lack of sleep, difficulty falling asleep or even interrupted sleep can negatively impact your mood. Nothing substitutes for a good night's rest. Since we all have 24 hours in one day, we get to choose how we slice and dice it to prioritize our sleep for sustained mental health.

Hands-on therapeutic touch such as acupuncture, massage, facials, manicures, and pedicures are beautiful ways to reinforce your emotional self-care.

Chapter 8 — Gut-brain connection

"Food can be the best medicine or the worst poison."

— Anonymous

You may wonder what a chapter about the gut has to do with mental health. The truth is a book about mental health that doesn't include a discussion about your gut is missing a fundamental link for wholesome mental health. And I would be remiss if I did not discuss the gut's role in your mental health.

There is a close connection between your gut and your brain. They 'speak' to each other. Your gut influences your brain, and vice versa; your brain 'speaks' to your gut. There is a reasonable explanation to understand how our gut and brain communicate with each other without using any complex scientific language. At the most basic level, it is imperative that you understand that gut health correlates with and is part of the process of achieving mental health. So, of course, I feel compelled to include gut health in this mental health book.

The wide range of emotions we feel as human beings can generally fit under the umbrella of four basic emotions: "Happy, sad, anger, and fear." However, each emotion has a spectrum from the lower end of the emotional expression to the extreme high end.

For example, on the low end of the happy spectrum, we may feel pleased and content, and the happy feeling can be evoked by a minor achievement, such as cleaning one's room after a long while or finishing that once old task. In contrast, on the high end of the happy spectrum, you feel exhilarated, exuberant, and joyful.

With anger on the low end, you may feel displeased and slighted or a mere annoyance and irritation; at someone; however, on the high end of the anger spectrum, you will be in a fit of rage, fury that can lead to physical violence.

On the low end of sadness emotional spectrum, you experience reduced joy and wouldn't care about things. While on the high end, one may feel so depressed that they neglect personal hygiene, experience changes in sleep, appetite, concentration, self-esteem, or energy levels, and no longer enjoy activities and interests they once used to enjoy.

With fear, on the low end, you may feel fright as when a person is suddenly startled by a loud noise behind them, while on the high end, you feel terror so incapacitating that you do not leave your home. You will consider everything dangerous outside your home.

Furthermore, between the extremes of the low and high ends, there are many emotional descriptors. These emotional descriptors are so vast that you may have difficulty describing your emotions, especially when you are experiencing more than one emotion simultaneously. This is not unusual since the three emotions of anger, fear, and sadness tend to hang out together. Where you see one of these emotions, you often experience the other. Sometimes one takes the lead, but the other two are closely attached. You know that you are experiencing more than one emotion when you say something like, "I don't know what it is that I'm feeling."

I mentioned in an earlier chapter that our emotions reside in our bodies. Our emotions have a physical address in our bodies. Just like you have a physical home address where you receive mail and packages, it is important to know the physical address for your emotions. It could be any part of your body and is unique to each of us. That physical location in your body gets tense when your emotions overwhelm your capacity to manage them. Now here is the bottom line, our emotions are also often experienced in our gut. You only need to take an intent look at how your gut responds to your emotions and the language you use to express your body sensations. We use expressions like I have a "gut feeling" about something or someone, or we use terms like "gut-wrenching;" these expressions did not just leap out of nowhere. We use them because when we feel anxious or afraid, we often feel it in our gut.

Children sometimes cry that they have upset stomachs or bellyaches when they feel stressed and anxious about doing something or going somewhere that threatens their emotional security, e.g., going to school. It happens with adults as well. The anxiety and dread you experience when you are tasked with public speaking or giving a presentation in front of a class or workshop cause a fluttering or 'butterflies' in your stomach; Whatever may be the cause of the anxiety, you will find a corresponding digestive system response with the full variety of physical symptoms, from belly-full laughter to knots in the stomach.

Scientists tell us that the gut has over 100 million nerve cells. Yes, you read that right; nerve cells are in your gut. Hence it is referred to as the second brain.

Before that, you may have thought that nerve cells are only found in the physical brain in your head, and you learned that your nervous system is comprised of the brain and spinal cord. And now you learn that there are nerve cells in your gut. This knowledge will aid you in understanding some of your gut-emotional symptoms.

You are already aware that when thinking about eating or having a favorite meal, the thought signals the digestive system to prepare with digestive enzymes to break down the bolus of food, so; you begin to salivate, and your gut rumbles in anticipation of the food before you. Just the thought of food activates the physiological response of the digestive system.

Just as the nerve cells in the brain in your head secrete biochemical substances, similarly, the nerve cells in your gut produce neurotransmitters and biochemical substances. These biochemical substances or neurotransmitters help with mood management. Examples of neurotransmitters include Dopamine and Serotonin; these hormones give feelings of well-being, optimism, peacefulness, and contentment. Low serotonin levels may evoke symptoms of anxiety, depression, irritability, etc.

When you understand that the foods you eat have a notable impact on your mental health, you begin to take charge and control the things you eat. Our digestive system starts with the mouth, and the food and drinks we consume either benefit or hurt the body. And since emotions are located, stagnated, and expressed in the body, it can be said that diet and emotions are two sides of the same coin. Therefore, pay attention to both; the gut and the brain.

The goal of having a good diet and lifestyle is that it also benefits and ameliorates our emotions; a good diet is one factor that can uplift the mood.

Reducing inflammation in the physical body is paramount because an inflamed gut can deteriorate the gut lining and leak minute food substances into the bloodstream. The technical word for this is 'intestinal permeability,' but more commonly, it is known as leaky gut. Food particles are not to enter the bloodstream, but when they do, because of a leaky gut, it sets in motion your immune system to attack the food as a foreign invader, which may further exacerbate a cascade of inflammatory cytokines degrading the integrity of physical health leading to physical illness. Physical illness negatively affects your mental health. A leaky gut can also be compared with the "leaky blood-brain barrier." It would need more than a few sentences to clarify the leaky gut and leaky blood-brain barrier in this chapter. However, what I want you to take away from this chapter is that gut and mental health are correlated. Thus, improved gut health leads to improved mental health.

There are reportedly over 100 trillion bacteria in the gut. These bacteria perform essential roles in keeping us healthy. When the delicate balance of this bacterial system in the gut is disrupted, it causes an imbalance known as gut dysbiosis. The disruption can occur for several reasons; some are within our control, and others are out of our control. For example, global environmental pollution, including air or water pollution, may be out of our control; however, we can limit its effect by focusing and working on the things we can control to reduce elevated levels of toxicity in our bodies. We can start managing our health (both physical and mental) by making wise decisions about the things we put on and into our bodies.

Managing our internal stress is also within our control, because increased and sustained stress levels correspond to increased and sustained levels of Cortisol in our bodies. Cortisol can be erosive to our internal organs at sustained elevated levels and can induce physical and, subsequently, mental/emotional problems. The cycle is that persistent stress may induce disease in the physical body, and this induction in the physical disease cycle will increase the existing stress. All this will become a perpetual ongoing cycle.

A common physical illness correlated with stress or anxiety is Irritable Bowel Syndrome (IBS). There is no specific test to diagnose IBS. However, its symptoms are generally correlated with increased anxiety and stress. The symptoms include abdominal pain and discomfort experienced at least once a week in the last three months. IBS symptoms are of three types: constipation-predominant, diarrhea-predominant, or mixed. If a mental health issue exhibits as a physical health issue, the first step to relief is to rule out any physiological or biological cause.

If a physical cause is ruled out, your doctor may recommend that you seek mental health counseling support to address any underlying cause that may be contributing to your symptoms. One way you can take charge of your health is by managing your stress levels.

In the next chapter, I will share some practical strategies you may begin to include in your diet and lifestyle to support your mental health journey.

Chapter 9 — Foods/Herbs For Mental Health

"Let food be your medicine and medicine your food."

—Hippocrates

"When the diet is wrong, medicine is of no use; when the diet is right, medicine is of no need."— Ayurvedic Proverb

Over the past centuries, standard agricultural practices have damaged soil structure, resulting in depleted soil nutrients and, consequently, poorer nutrients in cultivated crops. Our foods have lost nutritional value compared with similar crops of long ago; for this reason, it has become necessary to supplement our diets with nutrients that we would have otherwise gotten from our food source in the past.

You might have heard the saying, you are what you eat, but it might be more accurate to say you are what your gut absorbs. If what we eat has limited nutritional value compared with the nutrient-dense counterpart of a century ago, then it is crucial to supplement our diets. The previous chapter had an aerial view of the importance of our gut health to our mental health; however, in this chapter, I offer some practical ways to support your mental health through your diet and lifestyle, including supplementation.

The nutraceutical industry is a zillion-dollar (emphasis mine) enterprise, and it seems like a new vitamin, supplement, micronutrient, amino acid or fatty-acid product is on the grocery shelves every month, in the form of capsules, pills, powders, oils, or liquid. With fancy marketing strategies, they urge you to buy the new promise of a more robust life. I am aware that just the sheer variety is overwhelming and confusing to anyone facing the shelves and deciding whether to buy it or not. Furthermore, the choice gets complicated between fancy packaging and a good product.

I shall not recommend product names or brands in this chapter, as my favorites may not be yours. However, I will offer basic guidelines to consider in your dietary lifestyle.

I have loved herbs and plant medicine for a long time. I love the way they contribute to one's health. I love the combination of their gentleness and powerhouse capacity in how they purposely address the deeper physical and mental/emotional issues. The herbs listed in this chapter are not an extensive list, to say the least; however, the list should be understood mostly as the common and readily available herbs useful in mental health.

It should also be in your best interest to work with a licensed professional with expertise and training in nutritional and herbal foods. These professionals will comprehensively assess your physical and mental health history and offer client-specific recommendations.

Every herb does not have the same safety profile. Some herbs can be taken for long periods, while others require limited use and a smaller dose. Some are safe for general use, while others need to be taken in drops-dosage because they are powerful, and beyond that, they can be toxic. Some herbs are contraindicated for pregnant women, while others are safe for pregnant and lactating women. Some herbs need to be prepared in a specific way to achieve and maximize their health benefits; some require the use of the entire plant for medicinal properties; while others require the use of a specific part of the plant, e.g., the root, bark, flowers, leaves, fruits, or berries. Some herbs have an affinity to different and specific body-organs, while others strengthen your whole-body system. There just isn't any way to cover the vast scope and depth of how herbs function, or to appropriately cover their mechanisms of actions because there is so much more to learn about these beneficial plants.

However, to honor the value of herbs and the need for herbal medicine in our physical and mental health, there needs to be a level of respect for herbs as we incorporate them into our lives. Using herbs carelessly might induce the opposite effect of what you hope to achieve, including exacerbating conditions unintentionally. This is the reason why I emphasized the importance of working with a licensed professional. This professional will consider your mental/emotional profile and your physical constitution before prescribing any botanical medicine.

Since there is no way that one chapter in this book can cover all the beneficial herbs in existence; and since the author does not possess any omniscient abilities to know every nuance of your physical health; your pharmaceutical drug regimen, or the consequence of drug-herb interactions or drug-drug-interactions that is specific to you, the reader; I have intentionally limited the list of herbs to the ones with the best safety profile that can be useful to you. I have listed them in categories for easy reference. You may notice that the same herb can also be found on multiple lists; this is the beauty of these miraculous plants.

The mindset of popping "a pill for every ill" or substituting an herb to 'fix' a medical problem is neither the intent nor goal of this discussion. The goal is to acquire overall well-being with appropriate dietary and lifestyle changes so that you can flourish and prosper in the areas of your physical and mental/emotional life. I also caution the reader to stop self-diagnosing and self-prescribing herbs or nutrients. Refrain from filling your medicinal pantry with stuff you got at a local health food store because it worked for a friend, or worse — you saw a commercial advertisement.

That said, there is a feedback loop between mental health and nutritional deficiencies. For example, anxiety or depression can result from nutritional deficiencies, which can also increase or exacerbate anxiety or depression. Be also aware that anxiety can be exacerbated with the intake of substances like caffeine or cannabis.

It is necessary that our dietary intake reflect satisfying amounts of nutrient-dense and colorful plant-foods; and supplementing to enhance our nutrient profile is also beneficial for our physical and mental health.

Since some readers may interpret the herbs and nutrients listed as recommendations, I'm required to say that none of these statements have been evaluated by the FDA or are meant to imply diagnoses, treatments or cures to prevent any disease. Always consult a professional healthcare provider.

Anti-Inflammatory

An inflamed body creates an environment for disease to establish a foothold. So increasing anti-inflammatory foods in your regular diet is necessary, as they help the body quench free radicals. They also have the potential to decrease brain and physical inflammation. The following are common anti-inflammatory foods/herbs:

Turmeric/Curcumin
Green tea
Resveratrol
Quercetin

Herbs that are useful for:

Attention Deficit Hyperactivity Disorder

Bacopa: increases memory, mood, and concentration

Brahmi/Water hyssop

Chamomilla: Do not use in pregnancy or during hypothyroidism

Gotu kola: Limit use in pregnancy

Kava kava: Avoid in the first trimester

Lemon balm: Avoid during pregnancy

Skullcap: Avoid during pregnancy

Anxiety

Oats

Brahmi/Water hyssop

California Poppy

Chamomile: Avoid in first-trimester pregnancy

Kava kava: Avoid in the first trimester. Contraindicated in liver inflammation or disease, Parkinson's disease, and alcohol use. Do not take high doses when operating machinery.

Lavender: May use the essential oil on your sleep pillow

Lemon balm: Avoid during pregnancy

Motherwort

Hops

Saffron

Skullcap: Avoid during pregnancy

Valerian: Some patients experience a stimulating effect

Vervain, Blue Vervain: Do not use during pregnancy

Ashwagandha

Mimosa

Depression

Eleuthero

Lemon Balm: Avoid during pregnancy

Oats

Rhodiola

St. John's Wort: Avoid pregnancy. Caution: Limit sun exposure with use. Drug-herb interactions can occur.

Vervain, Blue Vervain: Do not use during pregnancy

Saffron

Fatigue

Brahmi/Water hyssop

Insomnia

California Poppy

Hops

Lavender: May use as essential oil on your sleep pillow

Motherwort

Passionflower: Limit the use during pregnancy

Rhodiola

Skullcap: Avoid during pregnancy

Valerian: Some experience a stimulating effect

Vervain, Blue Vervain: Do not use during pregnancy.

Panic Attacks

Kava kava: Avoid in the first trimester of pregnancy.

Restlessness

California Poppy

Hops

Kava kava: In anxiety, panic attack, and restlessness: It relaxes your body and makes you more mentally alert. Avoid in the first trimester.

Motherwort

Chamomile: Avoid in first-trimester pregnancy

Stress

Ashwagandha

Eleuthero

Gotu Kola: Limit use in pregnancy

Kava kava

Rhodiola

Nutraceuticals

A general guide would be to choose a single comprehensive multivitamin supplement with over 300 natural ingredients containing both Fulvic and Humic. This will be a superb addition to your multivitamin intake. Supplements that contain Fulvic and Humic generally maximize absorption. Taking one such supplement is better than trying to take individual vitamins and minerals, of which the sheer amount can be overwhelming.

Gut Support

Implementing any of the following can start you on the journey to supporting your mental health:

Probiotics: Lactobacillus Sacromyces b; Lacto sporogenes (this survives the stomach acid); re-balancing and repopulating the gut is a task we can undertake with some simple changes in our diet and lifestyle habits.

Soluble fiber

Inulin

Legumes

Fruits and nuts:

Foods that help stabilize mood and can increase serotonin:

Dietary tryptophan: Foods: soy, milk, turkey, whole grains.

Amino acid neurotransmitters: GABA, Taurine, glycine, inositol (Primarily Inhibitory), and Theanine.

GABA: can help reduce anxiety, stress, insomnia, hyperactivity, and mania, and it lowers blood pressure.

Zinc increases GABA in the brain. Adding L. Arginine to GABA is better

Taurine: Helps sleep, anxiety, and hyperactivity: Taurine + GABA + B6

L-tryptophan, 5HTP

Supplements

EFAs: Omega-3 fatty acids

Zinc

Selenium

B6, B12, folate

Vitamin C, E, antioxidants

Magnesium (Mg): There are over 300 biochemical reactions that need Mg to function properly in the body. Mg also helps to relax muscles. Excess may cause diarrhea.

Glycine

Phosphatidylserine

Treatment of Depression

Vitamins B12 and B6, folic acid, and omega-3 fatty acids supplementation

Hypericum (St John's Wort). Also used in Major Depressive Disorder. Caution as drug-herb interactions can occur.

SUPPLEMENTS FOR ADHD

Multiple vitamin-minerals

B6 (P5P)

Magnesium

Zinc

Essential fatty acids

Omega 3

Krill oil

Phosphatidylserine

Chapter 10 — Cannabidiol (CBD) And Mental Health

This is not the last chapter because of the confusion around the laws of its use or because of its vilified past or controversies of it once being labeled as a gateway drug, a highly addictive substance, or contraband. Nor is it because some states on the continent of North America have fully legalized it for medicinal and recreational use and decriminalized its status, while other states have not or have mixed legal status. Even though its use is becoming increasingly favorable in the United States, evidenced by its legalized medical status in many states. There is still no federal law that authorizes its legal use; as such, it is federally illegal to use unless it is within a state that has legalized its use. However, medicinal cannabis is recognized by the US Drug Enforcement Agency (DEA) and the Controlled Substance Act of 1970 as a Schedule 1 controlled substance, essentially because of its potential for abuse; so, the reader must become familiar with their state's laws that either regulate or unauthorized its use.

The history of the cannabis plant traces back to 6000BCE as an agricultural crop in China. In the United States, it was once used as medicine in the 19th and 20th centuries; and was listed among other medicines in the United States Pharmacopoeia in the early 1850s.

With the passage of the Marijuana Tax Act in 1937, there were new restrictions on how cannabis was to be sold and used. Then in the early 1940s, cannabis was removed from the list of medicines.

Then, with the passage of two additional Acts, namely the Boggs Act (1951) and the Narcotic Control Act (1956), legal penalties were applied for having it in your possession. Added to this, when the Controlled Substances Act was enacted in 1970, there was another layer of criminalization to having it in your possession.

Its re-emergence came in 1996 with the 'Compassionate Use Act' when the state of California allowed botanical cannabis to be used for medicinal purposes, but it had to be under a physician's supervision. Many states thereafter followed California's lead enacting legislations of their own to govern medicinal cannabis use, including its sale and distribution. Some of the following states have either decriminalized the use or sale of cannabis altogether, while others have legalized its use for adult recreation with some guidelines. As of this writing, the current list of states includes the following:

Alaska
Arizona
California
Colorado
Illinois
Maine
Massachusetts
Michigan
Montana
Nevada
New Jersey
New Mexico
New York
Oregon
South Dakota
Vermont
Virginia
Washington

Truth be told, I chose this chapter to be the last chapter because of the technical language I cannot avoid. So, let's just get the technical definition stuff out of the way before discussing CBD and mental health. The terms to differentiate are cannabis, Cannabinoids, endocannabinoid, cannabidiol (CBD), and Tetrahydrocannabinol (THC).

Cannabis

Cannabis is a plant that produces a substance with over 500 chemical compounds. The two most widely known compounds are Cannabidiol (CBD) and Tetrahydrocannabinol (THC).

There are two strains of the Cannabis plant, namely 'Sativa and Indica.' The Cannabis sativa strain has a lower concentration of THC but is high in cannabidiol content. On the other hand, the Cannabis indica strain has a higher content of THC.

Cannabis is often referred to as marijuana and occasionally used interchangeably; however, they are not the same. Though marijuana comes from the cannabis plant and mainly from the Sativa strain, it is only part of the plant product and not the plant. And the part of the plant from which it is extracted has significant levels of THC; thus, marijuana has a psychoactive chemical substance called THC. The THC induces a hallucinogenic effect leading to the altered mental state of feeling "high." The plants that contain minimal THC are often referred to as industrial hemp instead of marijuana and are cultivated for medicinal purposes or other use, e.g., to produce products like rope, cloth, and paper.

Cannabinoids

These are the group of substances from the cannabis plant that is believed to regulate how our cells communicate and interact with each other in the brain. The main cannabinoids are tetrahydrocannabinol (THC) and cannabidiol (CBD).

The US Food and Drug Administration has not approved the cannabis plant for medicine; however, they have approved certain drugs that contain individual cannabinoids. These drugs either include purified forms of CBD or synthetic forms of THC for the treatment of conditions such as seizures related to two rare and severe forms of epilepsy; it is also used for nausea and vomiting from chemotherapy and for people with HIV/AIDS suffering from loss of appetite and weight loss.

Endocannabinoid & Cannabidiol (CBD):

Our body produces its own cannabinoids, referred to as endogenous cannabinoids or endocannabinoids. These endocannabinoids are found throughout our bodies, including our nervous system, immune cells, organs, glands, and tissues.

The body's endocannabinoid system is essential for life, and their deficiency in our bodies may be responsible for some health disorders like depression, schizophrenia, migraines, or irritable bowel syndrome (IBS). Our endocannabinoid receptors can be stimulated by plant-based cannabinoids in cannabis.

The main endocannabinoid that we know of is called 'Anandamide.' Anandamide has a similar chemical structure to THC. When THC interacts with our main endocannabinoid receptors, it gives the 'high' that is generally associated with the use of cannabis. CBD, however, does not have the psychoactive component of THC, i.e., it does not produce the 'high' feeling, but it is reputed to have significant therapeutic benefits with specific dosing and preparations. These benefits include the following:

Anxiety-reduction
Chronic pain reduction
Insomnia
Anti-epileptic
Antipsychotic
Anti-inflammatory
Insomnia
Neuroprotective: (it protects our brain cells (neurons)

While some studies contradict others, and while there is little research on some mental health issues, there seems to be an agreement that CBD may be helpful with some mental health disorders, e.g., generalized anxiety, social anxiety, PTSD, difficulty staying asleep, and nightmares.

Forms of CBD

Because of the legal status of CBD in many states, there have been a plethora of dispensaries offering a variety of products that can be smoked, vaporized, or ingested. Various forms of CBD include the following:

Oils
Edibles, e.g., gummies
Capsules
Tinctures
Similarities between CBD & THC
They both interact with endogenous cannabinoids and can:
Relieve pain
Reduce nausea
Ease migraine
Reduces anxiety
Act as anti-inflammatory
Help with insomnia

Differences between CBD & THC include (but are not limited to):

THC is illegal at the federal level
Consuming THC makes you high, while CBD does not

THC show up on drug test, while CBD may or may not show up

THC is not known to diminish depression or decrease seizures, while CBD does

THC increases appetite, and CBD does not do that.

Adverse side effects of THC may include:

Slower response times

Issues with coordination

Memory loss

Increased heart rate

Red eyes and dry mouth

Vomiting

Safety concerns include (but are not limited to):

Cannabis use disorder: with symptoms of withdrawal, lack of control, neglect of personal and professional duties and responsibilities

It can result in a lower birth rate if smoked during pregnancy

It can cause dizziness if you stand suddenly, resulting in serious falls

Severe mental illness, e.g., psychotic disorders if you are pre-disposed to schizophrenia

Reports of contamination for some cannabis/cannabidiol products

Recurrent vomiting for high-dosing long-term users.

Lastly, it seems likely that the robust discussion on the use of botanical cannabis will continue. More research is needed for sure, but the fact that some states have allowed it for medical necessity, it would be in your best interest to have a consultation with your doctor to discuss whether adding CBD would augment your treatment plan.

To remain in compliance with state laws, your physician can either certify or recommend you for treatment, but they cannot prescribe cannabis legally and remain in compliance with federal or state laws.

In order to receive a state-issued medical marijuana card, there needs to be a medical necessity. Qualifying diagnoses may differ between and among states; however, the medical conditions eligible for the card include some or all of the following:

Alzheimer's disease

HIV/AIDS

Amyotrophic Lateral Sclerosis (ALS)

Cancer
Inflammatory Bowel Disease (IBD)
Glaucoma
Multiple sclerosis
Parkinson's disease
Post-Traumatic Stress Disorder (PTSD)
Severe or chronic pain
Severe or chronic nausea
Seizures
Skeletal muscle spasticity, e.g., MS
Wasting syndromes, e.g., anorexia, cachexia.

Chapter 11 — Conclusion

You can achieve and maintain robust mental health in your everyday life.

It is not elusive to anyone who pursues it. It is available to all. It is available to you. You may need additional therapeutic support to get off the path where you are emotionally exhausted and physically drained all the time, but tomorrow can be better than today with support.

The first and most important step is reaching out to get the help and support you need and deserve.

Achieving and maintaining your goal to live emotionally healthy lives is the work we all have to do. No one gets a free pass. We each have to make a renewed commitment to choose our mental health every day. Neglecting it would keep us stuck in anger, sadness, fear, or some variation of distress or dysfunction where we are tired of being tired.

Just like we attend to our physical hygiene daily, we need to attend to our emotional hygiene.

Any noble goal requires intentional focus and discipline to practice the set of required skills to nurture it. It is not a sprint; it's a journey, and it evolves and gets easier over time.

God designed us to thrive, flourish, prosper and have and live abundant lives with overflowing joy.

For these reasons, I have chosen to support your mental health journey by offering this 'counseling-in-a-book' to help you become the best version of yourself.

If our paths ever were to meet in a counseling or healing space, my intention for you would be the same one that is found in the Biblical text of 3 John 2:2:

"I wish above all things that you prosper and be in health even as your soul prospers."

References

http://www.ncbi.nlm.nih.gov/pubmed/19388520[1]

http://www.ncbi.nlm.nih.gov/pubmed/20215757

http://www.ncbi.nlm.nih.gov/pubmed/18843608

http://www.ncbi.nlm.nih.gov/pubmed/16808927

https://www.ncbi.nlm.nih.gov/pmc/articles/PMC5312634

Eye Movement Desensitization (EMDR) 'EMDRIA-approved Basic Training

Multi-channel Eye Movement Integration (MEMI) Certification

Bible.com

1. http://www.ncbi.nlm.nih.gov/pubmed/19388520

www.ingramcontent.com/pod-product-compliance
Lightning Source LLC
LaVergne TN
LVHW090429210926
848480LV00002B/746